OTHER SCIENTIFIC AMERICAN FOCUS BOOKS
Medication of the Mind
Cosmic Collisions
The Language of Animals
The Structure of the Universe
The New Media and the Future of Communications

OF
MIND
AND
BODY

LINDA WASMER SMITH

Foreword by Alice D. Domar, Ph.D.

A SCIENTIFIC AMERICAN FOCUS BOOK

An Owl Book

Henry Holt and Company
New York

Henry Holt and Company, Inc.
Publishers since 1866
115 West 18th Street
New York, New York 10011

Henry Holt® is a registered trademark
of Henry Holt and Company, Inc.

Published in Canada by Fitzhenry & Whiteside Ltd.
195 Allstate Parkway, Markham, Ontario L3R 4T8.

Library of Congress Cataloging-in-Publication Data
Smith, Linda Wasmer.
Of mind and body / Linda Wasmer Smith;
foreword by Alice Domar.—1st ed.
p.   cm. — (A Scientific American Focus book)
"An Owl Book."
Includes bibliographical references and index.
1. Medicine, Psychosomatic.   2. Mind and body.   3. Mind and body therapies.
I. Title.   II. Series.
RC49.S54   1996
616'.001'9—dc20   96-40995

ISBN 0-8050-4030-7
ISBN 0-8050-4031-5 (An Owl Book: pbk.)

First edition—1997

Photo credits are on page 144.

Editorial and production services:
G&H SOHO, Inc., Hoboken, NJ

Printed in the United States of America
All first editions are printed
on acid-free paper. ∞

10 9 8 7 6 5 4 3 2 1
10 9 8 7 6 5 4 3 2 1 (pbk.)

To the memory of my two mothers
Nettie Wasmer (1927–1995)
and
Anne Smith (1909–1990)
who taught me much about life through their deaths.

ACKNOWLEDGMENTS

At about the same time that I signed the contract to write this book, my mother's health, which had been poor for some months, began a precipitous decline. Nothing I learned from the hundreds of documents read and the dozens of experts interviewed contained a magic formula to save her. She died almost exactly two months before my manuscript was completed. I'm saddened that she'll never be able to read it, comment on this point, and quibble with that. Nevertheless, the simultaneous passage through the sharing of a death and the birthing of a book has taught me many useful things—about the value of hope and the cruelty of false promises, and about quality of living and dying as compared to quantity of life. Therefore, my deepest debt is to my mother, and my greatest wish is that her lessons be reflected in the pages to come.

In addition, I would like to thank the numerous researchers and clinicians who shared their own hard-won insights so freely. Many of these generous souls are mentioned by name in the text. Among those whose names are omitted due to space constraints, but whose contributions are no less appreciated, are Ed Etzel, Ed.D., of West Virginia University; Mary Gregerson, Ph.D., of George Washington University in Washington, D.C.; Jessie Gruman, Ph.D., of the Center for the Advancement of Health in Washington, D.C.; Roy Hall, M.D., of Cancer Treatment Centers of America in Northbrook, Ill.; Yutaka Haruki, Ph.D., of Waseda University in Japan; Brad Hatfield, Ph.D., of the University of Maryland; Jennifer Haythornthwaite, Ph.D., of Johns Hopkins University in Baltimore; Blair Justice, Ph.D., of the University of Texas in Houston; Ben Kline, Ph.D., of Lovelace Medical Center in Albuquerque, N.M.; Kenneth Klivington, Ph.D., of the Fetzer Institute in Kalamazoo, Mich.; Robert Kloner, M.D., Ph.D., of the University of Southern California; Yoshitake Konno, Ph.D., of Bunkyo University in Japan; Peg Krach, Ph.D., of Purdue University in West Lafayette, Ind.; Daniel Landers, Ph.D., of Arizona State University; François Lespérance, M.D., of the University of Montreal; Donald Liggett, Ph.D., of Gig Harbor, Wash.; Lewis Mehl-Madrona, M.D., Ph.D., of the University of Vermont; Nancy Moore, Ph.D., of St. Charles Medical Center in Bend, Ore.; Gosaku Naruse, Ph.D., of Kyushu University in Japan; Theodore Pincus, M.D., of Vanderbilt University in Nashville; Ronald Price, Ph.D., of Northern Illinois University; Richard Sherman, Ph.D., of Madigan Army Medical Center in Tacoma, Wash.; Erin Sommerville, of the Simonton Cancer Center in Pacific Palisades, Calif.; Francisco Varela, Ph.D., of the Ecole Polytechnique in Paris; William Whitehead, Ph.D., of the University of North Carolina; and Fredrick Wigley, M.D., of Johns Hopkins University.

I would also like to extend my deep gratitude to David Sobel at Henry Holt.

Linda Wasmer Smith

C O N T E N T S

**hen** we watch a scary movie, our bodies react as if *we* were the one in danger. Moviegoers watching "The Silence of the Lambs," for example, probably were aware of their hearts pounding, their hands sweating, and even their breath getting short when the dreaded Hannibal Lector got loose. Any rational person *knows* that the movie scene is not real life, but when the brain notes a risky situation, there is an immediate physical reaction. So, although it was the character played by Jodie Foster who was in danger, *our* bodies were ready to meet the physical challenge of being attacked. This is the mind-body connection in action.

There are countless examples of the mind-body connection in real life, ranging from the rise in blood pressure of most women as they wait in their gynecologist's office to the ability of a handful of men to raise an overturned car to save the life of an accident victim. What goes on in our minds can have a direct and immediate impact on our bodies (and vice versa—when you are experiencing a bout with the flu, do you feel happy and lighthearted?). In fact, there is a constant flow of information, in both directions, between the mind and the body. Our thoughts and emotions can have a direct impact on our immune system, our reproductive organs, and our entire nervous system. We are more likely to catch a cold when we are stressed than when life is calmer; women who are depressed prior to undergoing high-tech infertility treatment are half as likely to get pregnant as nondepressed women; and diabetics have more difficulty controlling their blood sugar levels when they are anxious. Chapters Two and Three provide clear explanations on how the mind/body connection works.

During the past ten years, scientific research has shown increasingly that as we learn more about the adverse impact of stress on our bodies and minds, learning how to *de*stress can lead to greater physical and psychological health. There is preliminary evidence that cancer patients who learn various relaxation and stress management skills (often called mind-body techniques) live longer than patients who do not learn these skills. People who practice relaxation and self-hypnosis prior to surgery have less postoperative pain, need fewer narcotics, and go home earlier than other patients. Even children can learn to use this approach to get healthier: research supports a mind-body approach to alleviating migraine headaches, test anxiety, and eating disorders in children and adolescents. Many more examples of the treatment of stress and the resultant distress are provided in Chapters Five through Seven.

Just as there are probably thousands of situations that cause us to feel distressed and anxious, there are many ways to achieve increased peace of mind. Techniques that elicit the relaxation response include meditation, progressive muscle relaxation, imagery, the first phase of hypnosis, autogenic training, and praying quietly. Biofeedback can be used to give patients physical proof that they can have some control over their bodies. In addition to relaxation techniques, there are many stress-management techniques that can be used both to treat symptoms and to try to prevent the development of disease. These include various forms of psychotherapy, group cognitive-behavioral therapy, writing about one's thoughts and feelings, doing volunteer work, spending time with supportive friends and family members, owning a pet, listening to music, exercising, and simply laughing. These experiences have been linked to shorter hospital stays for patients with hip fractures, reduced death rates in melanoma patients, improved immune function in HIV+ men, decreased risk of developing heart disease, decreased anxiety and depression, and increased pain tolerance, to name a few examples.

It is important to remember, however, that the mind is not the only entity that can have an effect on the body. People get cancer not because they thought "wrong" thoughts but because of a combination of genetic and environmental factors. The presumed existence of the Type C, cancer-prone personality is still very much under investigation. Heart disease can be caused by a genetic predisposition, a high-fat diet, smoking, a sedentary lifestyle, diabetes, as well as the so-called Type A personality of hostile behavior.

One can use the mind-body connection to enhance one's health, to decrease symptoms, and to possibly decrease or delay death rates of certain diseases. However, this approach should always be used as a complement to modern medicine. The *combination* of mind-body medicine as well as traditional Western medicine may very well be the best medicine of all.

—Alice D. Domar, Ph.D.
Division of Behavioral Medicine, Mind/Body Medical Institute
Deaconess Hospital
Harvard Medical School

Mind-Body
Medicine

Glenda is walking her dog among the dusty bear grass and prickly cactus at the base of the Sandia Mountains on the east side of Albuquerque, but her mind's eye is looking inward. As her West Highland terrier tugs at its leash, the special education teacher imagines that the small white dog is a white blood cell poised to attack the cancer in her body. It's a technique she learned from a best-selling book and honed at a well-known cancer center. Perhaps, she thinks, such healing images combined with chemotherapy treatments can give her that critical edge in the life-and-death struggle against non-Hodgkin's lymphoma.

 erhaps. Certainly this is the kind of feel-good story that is repeatedly seen in popular books and magazine articles and heard on talk shows. As it happens, a year after her initial diagnosis, Glenda's cancer is now in remission. However, no one can predict what the future may hold—or what role this kind of imagery exercise may play in the final outcome. Yet Glenda, like a growing number of Americans today, is convinced that the link between mind and body is a powerful one that can be exploited to treat and prevent illness and enhance wellness.

The recent upsurge in public interest in what has come to be known as mind-body medicine has been swift and strong. A landmark 1993 study, published in the esteemed *New England Journal of Medicine,* was led by internist David Eisenberg, M.D., of Harvard Medical School. Eisenberg and his fellow researchers found that a third of a national sample of 1,539 adults said they had used at least one unconventional medical therapy within the past year. Most popular were relaxation techniques, which had been used in the last 12 months by 13 percent of those interviewed. Among other therapies tried by

> Relaxation techniques such as meditation are among the most popular types of mind-body treatment.

at least 1 percent of the respondents were imagery, spiritual healing, self-help groups, biofeedback, and hypnosis.

Mind-body medicine is an approach that sees mental phenomena such as thoughts and emotions as being central to the body's physical health. Treatments based on the interconnectedness of body and mind include, in addition to those cited above, meditation, psychotherapeutic techniques, music therapy, and humor therapy. An older, and still often-used, term for this field is *psychosomatic medicine.*

One ground-breaking study that assessed the effectiveness of some such treatments was directed by Stanford psychiatrist David Spiegel, M.D. Back in 1976, 86 women with advanced breast cancer were randomly assigned to either an experimental group or a control (comparison) group. For a year afterward, both groups received standard medical care, but only those in the experimental group also got weekly supportive group therapy with self-hypnosis training for pain control. A decade later, the researchers tracked down what had become of these patients. They found that the women who had taken part in support groups had lived an average of 18 months longer than their counterparts who had not—a finding that is especially striking since Spiegel's original goal was actually to disprove the idea that psychological factors could influence the course of cancer. (This study is discussed in greater detail in Chapter Six.)

Taken together, the various mind-body interventions are one aspect of *alternative medicine,* an umbrella term for practices that fall outside conventional Western medicine. In addition to mind-body therapies, these include such things as acupuncture, herbal medicine, homeopathy, massage therapy, and alternative diets.

To more fully explore these kinds of practices, Congress established an Office of Alternative Medicine within the National Institutes of Health in 1992. Of the first 30 grants awarded by that office, 10 went to researchers investigating mind-body control. Among the wide-ranging projects that received this funding were a study of biofeedback and relaxation for diabetes at the Medical College of Ohio, a study of guided imagery for asthma at Lenox Hill Hospital in New York City, and a study of hypnosis for chronic low back pain at the Virginia Polytechnic Institute and State University.

Rather than calling mind-body approaches alternative, some people prefer the term *complementary medicine.* This highlights the fact that such therapies are best used as an adjunct to mainstream medical care instead of a replacement for it.

How Conventional Wisdom Became Unconventional

Approaches deemed alternative in the present-day United States might well be the norm in another time or place, notes Marc Micozzi, M.D., Ph.D., a scientist trained as both a physician and an anthropologist who is director of the National Museum of Health and Medicine in Washington, D.C. "Even though we Westerners have been thinking of the mind and body as separate for several generations now, that's really an artificial separation," he says. "In many cultures, the whole concept of mind-body medicine would be meaningless, since you can't put the mind and body back together if you never split them."

Historians trace this intellectual rift to René Descartes, an influential seventeenth-century French

French philosopher René Descartes.

philosopher. Descartes was a dualist who thought the universe consisted of two basic elements: matter and mind. In this view, our minds belong to the spiritual sphere, while our bodies are part of the physical world of science. Initially, this separation gave medical scientists the freedom to experiment on the human body, while preserving for the church the realm of the mind. It eventually gave rise to *biomedicine,* the style of medicine now practiced by doctors with M.D. degrees, which has been the dominant medical system in the United States since the mid-1800s. Biomedical scientists came to believe that, given almost any affliction, they could eventually find a physical cause such as a bacterium, virus, or chemical imbalance. The problem could then be corrected with the appropriate vaccine or drug.

In the age of AIDS and cancer, however, this view can seem oversimplified. Many physicians and patients alike are embracing a broader view of healing as the restoration of balance in the natural forces within the body. Health systems based on this concept sprang up in ancient times in Greece, China, and India. While the Greek system was later overwhelmed by the Western scientific revolution, those in China and India have survived to modern times. "Today Asian medicine makes no distinction between body and mind in its approach to health and healing," says Micozzi. "The concept of a mind-body split just doesn't exist there. They don't know what we're talking about."

The Body Has a Mind of Its Own

By the 1930s, cracks in the foundations of strict biomedicine were already starting to appear. American psychiatrist Franz Alexander, M.D., built a framework for psychosomatic medicine with his astute observation that certain physical conditions seem to be strongly associated with emotional upset. As Alexander wrote in 1939, "many chronic disturbances are not caused by external, mechanical, chemical factors or by microorganisms, but by the continuous functional stress arising during the everyday life of the organism in its struggle for existence."

The traumatic events of World War II brought this connection to the forefront, as military doctors began reporting cases of what were called *organ neuroses*—conditions of the heart or digestive organs that were apparently caused by emotional disturbances. By the 1950s, the list of

Among residents of war-torn Sarajevo, stress has taken a heavy toll on both body and mind.

suspected *psychosomatic diseases*—conditions believed to be worsened by psychological stress—included asthma, high blood pressure, rheumatoid arthritis, peptic ulcers (ulcers of the stomach or upper small intestine), ulcerative colitis (ulcerating inflammation of the colon), neurodermatitis (skin inflammation associated with emotional disturbance), and hyperthyroidism (overactivity of the thyroid gland).

In the 1990s, we're still learning the hard way how chronic severe stress affects the human mind and body. This is shown by the emergence of a so-called Sarajevo syndrome, a cluster of stress-related psychological and physical symptoms that seem to be on the rise among residents of that beleaguered city. And researchers are still working to establish which diseases really are caused or worsened by stress. Any cause-and-effect relationship has not proved to be as straightforward as once assumed. For example, despite the long-standing reputation of peptic ulcers as a stress-induced disease, doctors now recognize that the *Helicobacter pylori* bacterium plays a major role in their development. Nevertheless, the impact of stress is pervasive. In fact, many popular mind-body therapies can actually be grouped under the heading of *relaxation techniques*—a broad term for therapeutic approaches used to counteract the body's stress response.

Holistic Healing and Hospitable Hospitals

However you categorize mind-body treatments, they tend to have certain basic characteristics in common. These fundamental principles include:

- **Holistic approach.** *Holism* is a philosophy which states that all aspects of a human being—physical, mental, emotional, and spiritual—are interrelated. Therefore, holistic health care providers focus not just on a specific symptom or disease, but on the person as a whole. Advocates point out that the words "whole," "heal," and "holy" share the same linguistic root.
- **Emphasis on healing.** Because of this focus on the total person, mind-body practitioners tend to stress bringing all sides of a person into better balance rather than just curing a particular disease or disorder. Therefore, the word "healing" is often used instead of "curing." Proponents claim it is possible for a person to be healed without the condition being cured.

- **Patient-centered care.** Given the multifaceted nature of each individual's needs, *patient-centered health care* recognizes that only a fraction of these can be met by medical professionals. People are encouraged to be active participants in their own health care rather than passive recipients. Of course, all mind-body therapies require a person's active involvement.

Consumers are starting to demand more sensitive and personalized treatment, and health care centers around the country are scrambling to respond. At St. Charles Medical Center in Bend, Oregon, for example, many rooms boast scenic mountain or desert views. Roving minstrels and rotating art shows help humanize the environment, while a "humor cart" helps relieve stress. There's even a wheelchair-accessible fishing pond designed for use by patients recovering from strokes or brain injuries.

In fact, there is some solid evidence that more hospitable hospitals really may promote faster healing. One classic 1984 study published in *Science* analyzed the records of 46 patients who had undergone gall bladder

Roving minstrels help create a welcoming atmosphere at St. Charles Medical Center in Bend, Oregon.

surgery at a suburban Pennsylvania hospital. Half had stayed in rooms with windows that looked out onto trees, while the other half had been in identical rooms that afforded only views of a brick wall. The patients with the trees view had shorter postoperative hospital stays, received fewer negative evaluative comments in the nurses' notes, and required fewer potent painkilling medications in the days just after surgery.

The Planetree Alliance: Quality Care for Patients and Families

At the forefront of the movement toward more humanistic medicine is the Planetree Health Care Alliance. Since its founding in 1978, this nonprofit organization has helped establish patient-centered programs at more than 20 hospitals across the United States and in Europe.

"Before coming to Planetree, I got written up once for not emptying a dirty linen cart out of an isolation room," says nurse Laura Gilpin, R.N., now director of hospital development for the San Francisco-based organization. "I never got written up for not spending time with a woman whose breast was going to be taken off the next morning. Clearly, in subtle and not-so-subtle ways, the hospital was communicating the message that caring and compassion were not valued. Planetree gave me permission to be the sort of caregiver I wanted to be."

The various Planetree units offer a number of features, big and small, aimed at creating a more nurturing environment. Patients wear their own pajamas

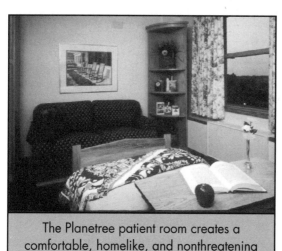

The Planetree patient room creates a comfortable, homelike, and nonthreatening atmosphere.

and sleep on flowered sheets. Visitors are allowed at all times, and friends and family can even cook for their loved ones in a specially provided kitchen. Interested family members are trained to serve as care partners, who learn how to perform such nursing tasks as changing dressings. Patients are also encouraged to educate themselves. To this end, the alliance operates several health resource centers around the country that are sources of health and medical information. In addition, an open-chart policy lets patients read their own records and even add their own comments.

People are free to pick and choose the services that seem most beneficial to them. Says Gilpin, "To me, what's important is to really personalize the care and make whatever is right for a given patient possible."

Bedside Manner 101 and Beyond

Of course, to make the most of holistic hospitals, you need more holistically oriented doctors to staff them. At medical schools nationwide, the push is on to provide training in mind-body and related approaches. For instance, in 1995, Harvard Medical School offered a continuing-education course for health professionals on alternative medicine that was billed as the first of its kind. Among the topics addressed were unconventional therapies for cancer and human immunodeficiency virus (HIV) infection.

While some mind-body classes concentrate on teaching specific techniques, such as hypnosis or biofeedback, others are essentially updated versions of Bedside Manner 101. Preliminary data presented by Michigan State University researchers at the 1995 meeting of the American Psychosomatic Society suggest that, not surprisingly, people may be happier with doctors who have learned to be more patient-centered. The researchers provided intensive training in psychosocial and humanistic aspects of medicine for 26 internal medicine and family practice residents. Instruction focused on such skills as giving top priority to patient needs, informing patients fully, and exhibiting warmth and confidence. Afterward, the patients of these residents expressed more satisfaction with their treatment than did the patients of other doctors.

Happier patients are one thing, but are they healthier, too? In fact, there's good evidence that expanding people's involvement in their own medical care can actually improve their prognosis. In one influential study,

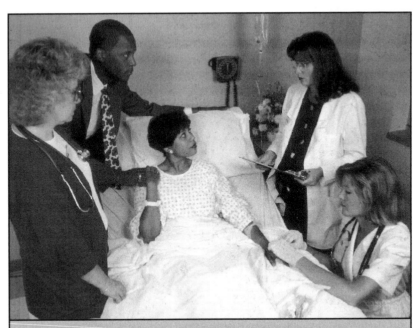

The art of medicine: Doctors today are rediscovering the healing power of a reassuring manner.

published in the *Annals of Internal Medicine* in 1985, researchers coached people with peptic ulcers in how to ask questions and negotiate decisions with their physicians. They also helped the patients read their own medical records. These patients were then compared to controls who had received only standard information about their condition. Audiotapes showed that the trained patients were twice as effective as the controls at getting information from their doctors. More importantly, patients in this group also reported fewer physical limitations six to eight weeks later.

Teaching New Docs Old Tricks

One of the most comprehensive programs in mind-body medical studies has been launched at the Georgetown University School of Med-

Opening the Lines of Communication

The American Academy of Family Physicians offers these tips for building a healthy partnership with your family or personal physician:

- **Put it in writing.** When you have an appointment, take along a written list to remind yourself of concerns you want to discuss.
- **Don't hesitate to ask.** It's your right to make knowledgeable decisions, so ask questions about anything you don't understand.
- **Do ask, do tell.** Be honest and specific about your symptoms. Be sure your doctor knows about all the medications you're taking.

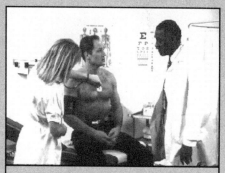

Be honest and specific about your symptoms.

icine. The driving force behind this innovative curriculum is James Gordon, M.D., who is also founder and director of the Center for Mind-Body Medicine in Washington, D.C.

"Each year, I offer an elective for first-year medical students called the Healing Partnership," says Gordon. "Everyone in the class has to keep a journal, because self-awareness should be the foundation of any approach to health care. . . . The students all meditate daily, and everybody engages in regular physical exercise."

Gordon also presents annual lectures on Illness as Personal Transformation and the Cultural and Social Context of Health and Illness. For second-year students, he offers a course called Introduction to Mind-Body Studies, which covers such topics as relaxation, meditation, self-hypnosis, biofeedback, and visual imagery. For fourth-year students in psychiatry, he supervises sessions in which such techniques are used with actual patients. Gordon also serves as a mentor to selected students who spend a month with him in his medical practice. In addition, he offers an extracurricular support group to help students cope with the stress of medical school.

The Georgetown program is regarded as a model for other medical schools across the nation. "There's a great deal of interest," says Gordon. "But most schools are just beginning something that has been evolving here since 1984. In many cases, they're starting out with a single elective course. Ultimately, they'll develop their own programs based on the talents and views of the faculty there."

The Hole in Holism

If there is a hole in holism, it is the lack of enough well-controlled studies such as those just mentioned to support its claims. Instead, there has been an overreliance on anecdotes. This tendency can be seen in a full-page magazine ad for a group of cancer treatment facilities that are described in their follow-up literature as providing mind-body care. "A Thousand Concerts Ago, I Had Cancer" reads the bold headline, and the text of the ad goes on to tell of one concert violinist's victory over breast cancer. At the bottom of the page, printed in tiny type, is this qualifier: "The effectiveness of any program depends on a variety of factors and differs from patient to patient." The truth is, while stories of an individual's dramatic recovery from disease may be inspiring, the results can't be generalized to the rest of us.

The traditional antidote to too much anecdote is the *experimental study*, in which a scientist changes only certain variables in a given situation to see what the outcome will be. Recently, compelling evidence for the connection between mind and body has begun to surface from three lines of investigation:

- **Epidemiological research.** *Epidemiology* is the study of populations to seek the causes of health and disease. In the context of mind-body medicine, such research shows what associations exist between particular emotions or beliefs and certain diseases in the population at large.

- **Physiological studies.** Once such associations have been identified, the next logical step is to explain why they occur. Physiological research explores biological and biochemical connections between the brain and the body's

Laboratory rats sometimes serve as stand-ins for a human condition under study in physiological research.

systems in the search for causal mechanisms. Some of this work is done in *animal models*—laboratory animals that function as stand-ins for the human disease or physiological change under investigation.

- **Clinical trials.** Knowledge gleaned from the two previous kinds of research is often applied to the development of mind-body techniques for treating or preventing disease. The effectiveness of such approaches can be assessed in *clinical trials,* in which an *experimental group* receives the treatment under investigation. An untreated *control group* is typically included for comparison. The gold standard in experimental medicine is the *controlled, randomized clinical trial,* in which the effect of a treatment is tested on two or more comparable, randomly selected groups.

The Stories of Our Lives

Although they are the ideal, controlled, randomized clinical trials pose an ethical dilemma that may make them impractical in some situations. On the one hand, researchers must be fairly certain of a treatment's safety and efficacy before they can subject people in an experimental group to it. On the other hand, once a treatment's effectiveness is well established, researchers can no longer in good conscience withhold it from people in a control group. Therefore, it's only during that limited time span when doctors believe a treatment is probably useful but aren't quite sure that it is a good candidate for controlled, randomized research. In addition, the wisdom of withholding even an unproven treatment from patients with no other hope is debatable.

Anyone can recognize the value of a good story in bringing home the human dimensions of a situation. That's why this book and others like it are sprinkled with individual examples. Scientists also realize that systematic observation is the very basis of their enterprise, and doctors know that much can be learned from the careful watching of a patient. That's why medical journals publish *case reports,* in which the specifics of individual cases are laid out in clinical detail.

However, as worthwhile as anecdotes and case histories may be, the information they provide has a serious drawback. The laws of probability tell us that seemingly rare coincidences are much more common than we generally believe. Think of it this way: The odds that any given person will win the lottery twice are extremely small. However, the odds that *someone, somewhere, someday* will be a double winner are quite good. Similarly, the odds that a small fraction of patients with an apparently fatal illness will inexplicably recover are also surprisingly high. If you happen to be one of those patients, your remarkable recovery may be due to the innovative treatment you've tried—or it may not. Without *controls* as a standard for comparison, there's no way to know whether you're a medical pathfinder or a statistical fluke.

Controlled, randomized research is not a panacea, but most scientists agree that some type of experimental study is usually the best tool for evaluating therapies. It's worth noting that all of the studies cited so far have been published since the mid-1980s. The number of well-designed studies of mind-body issues has grown rapidly in recent years. We'll examine the results in the chapters to come.

All in Your Mind:
Emotions, Beliefs, and Health

BOSTON, March 1994—The retired minister was at home in his second-floor apartment when heavily armed police officers on a drug raid suddenly burst in without warning. They chased the 75-year-old into his bedroom and wrestled him to the floor. Rev. Accelyne Williams suffered a fatal heart attack, which the Boston Globe *reported was "apparently induced by emotional stress." Tragically, the police later conceded that they had accidentally barged into the wrong apartment in the four-story building.*

ALBUQUERQUE, February 1995—One of Ruth Lindemann's greatest fears was that she would die first, leaving her ailing husband of more than 50 years alone in the nursing home where both were living. But at 10:10 one Wednesday morning, Herbert Lindemann suffered a fatal stroke. Sixty-five minutes later, Ruth, who had been suffering from breast cancer, drew her last breath as well. One of the couple's daughters told the Albuquerque Journal, *"It was as if they were able to choose their deaths."*

n an intuitive level, our culture seems to recognize that psychological phenomena such as feelings and thoughts can have a significant impact on physical health. Consider the commonness of such expressions as "scared to death" and "worried sick," and think of all the stories you've heard about people who exercise the "will to live" or die from a "broken heart." Today scientists are finally gathering hard evidence to support the existence of this long-suspected mind-body link.

One way to test this connection would be to observe different minds at work within the same body. To some degree, scientists have been able to do just that by observing people with multiple personality disorder.

Strong emotions have long been thought to exert a powerful influence on physical health. (Pablo Picasso, *Weeping Woman*. 1937. Tate Gallery, London.)

As the name implies, victims of this rare condition develop two or more personalities, one of which is dominant at any given time. Over the years, therapists have noted, for example, that one personality may be allergic to cats, while another remains unaffected.

Nicholas Hall, Ph.D., a professor of psychiatry and behavioral medicine at the University of South Florida, recently described the case of a woman who claimed more than 200 distinct personalities. In a unique study, Hall and his colleagues inserted a catheter into this woman's vein and took several blood samples over a four-hour period as she switched from one personality state to another. The blood was then checked for measures of immune system function, which turned out to differ markedly among the personalities. In a control subject without multiple personality disorder, the same measures showed little variability.

The woman in Hall's study seemed to meet all the criteria to qualify as a true case of multiple personality disorder. But she also clearly enjoyed the attention she and her many personalities received. What if she exaggerated certain characteristics to please the researchers during the study? As a practical matter, it may not have made much difference whether or not she was "acting," because either way, her immune function changed.

An interesting line of investigation pursued by both Hall and researchers elsewhere involves professional actors who intentionally arouse short-term emotional changes in themselves. Margaret Kemeny, Ph.D., a psychologist at the University of California in Los Angeles, has noted that Method-trained actors make a living by using their own memories and sensations to artificially create realistic emotional experiences. In a 1994 study, when Kemeny and her colleagues checked the blood of Method actors before and after they elicited positive or negative moods, the researchers found that mood changes consistently affected immune function.

Quick on the Trigger

The idea that sudden extreme emotional distress can even lead to death dates back at least to biblical times. Consider a Bible story that is recorded in Chapter 5 of the book of Acts. A man named Ananias was severely reprimanded by the apostle Peter for dishonestly withholding

Some victims of the 1994 Los Angeles earthquake may have been literally "scared to death."

part of the proceeds from a land sale. Ananias "hearing these words fell down, and gave up the ghost." Three hours later, his wife, Sapphira, still unaware of what had happened, committed the same dishonest act and was also severely chastised for it. She, likewise, dropped dead on the spot.

Can strong emotional reactions really trigger potentially fatal heart attacks? A study led by Murray Mittleman, M.D., recently tried to answer that question. "Many other investigators have looked at long-term risk factors for heart disease, such as smoking, blood pressure, and blood cholesterol," says Mittleman, an instructor of medicine at Harvard Medical School and New England Deaconess Hospital, who presented his findings at the 1994 meeting of the American Heart Association. "But we're more interested in what the immediate precipitants are."

The 53-hospital study by Mittleman and his colleagues included 1,623 men and women, who were interviewed within a few days of suffering a heart attack. The patients were asked to rate their own anger level during the two hours immediately preceding the attack on a seven-point scale ranging from "calm" to "furious and enraged." These anger scores were then compared to the patients' self-ratings of their usual frequency and intensity of angry outbursts over the past year. The researchers found that the average risk of having a heart attack was increased by 2.3 times during the two hours following the onset of moderate or greater anger.

The evidence for a link between intense fear and sudden death is no less convincing. Nature provided a stark demonstration in the form of the 1994 earthquake that struck the Los Angeles area. This was the topic of a paper presented at the 1995 meeting of the American College of Cardiology by two doctors from Good Samaritan Hospital in Los Angeles. The cardiologists reviewed causes of death listed by the coroner's office and found that, on the day of the quake, the risk of death from heart attack did indeed go up compared to days in previous years.

A Date with Death

Popular belief has also long held that people may have some control over the timing of their deaths. Take the example of 78-year-old Leon Day, a star pitcher in baseball's Negro Leagues during the 1930s and 1940s, who died after a long illness on March 13, 1995. Day's sister told the Associated Press that she believed her brother had clung to life until after a committee voted on whether to induct him into baseball's Hall of Fame. Day was elected on March 7. Six days later, he was dead.

Could cases such as this one be more than mere coincidence? Over the past half-century, several studies have found a correlation between dates of death and personally significant symbolic occasions, an effect labeled the *anniversary reaction.* These symbolic occasions can take the form of either "deadlines" or "lifelines." A deadline is a dreaded event. For example, some research suggests that a person may sicken and die upon reaching the age at which a parent died.

In contrast, lifelines are eagerly anticipated events. Legend has it that death is sometimes postponed until after such happy occasions. A study led by David Phillips, Ph.D., a sociologist at the University of California in San Diego, tested this notion by looking at deaths among Californians of Chinese descent in relation to the Harvest Moon Festival. The central role in this important Chinese holiday is assumed by the senior woman in a household, who takes charge of fixing an elaborate meal and directs the work of her daughters and daughters-in-law. The researchers found that older Chinese women died at a much lower rate than would be predicted by chance during the week before the festival, while mortality rose to a level well above the expected rate during the week afterward. This dip/peak effect, where some deaths seemed to be temporarily put on hold, was not seen in older Chinese men or young Chinese women.

The ABCs of Personality Type

Within an individual with multiple personality disorder, there is sometimes one personality that is singled out as "the healer," which appears to have fewer symptoms than the others. Among groups of mentally healthy people, there are also certain behavior types that seem to be more or less disease-prone than others. The best known of these are referred to alphabetically as Types A, B, and C.

The pioneers in this field were Meyer Friedman, M.D., and Ray Rosenman, M.D., who coined the term *Type A behavior pattern* to describe a cluster of personality traits, including excessive competitive drive, aggressiveness, impatience, and a harrying sense of time urgency. *Type B behavior pattern* refers to people who do not display these qualities. Back in the 1950s, the two cardiologists first began to suspect that there might be an association between the Type A complex of traits and coronary heart disease. In their 1974 book *Type A Behavior and Your Heart*, Friedman and Rosenman recount how one early clue came from an upholsterer called in to fix the chairs in their waiting room. The workman was curious about what kinds of patients the doctors treated, since only the front edges of the chair seats had been worn out. Apparently, these were the sorts of people who were literally "on the edge of their seats" much of the time, impatiently awaiting life's latest twist.

In 1960–1961, Friedman, Rosenman, and their coworkers undertook a major study that demonstrated the importance of Type A behavior as a risk factor for coronary heart disease. Over 3,000 initially healthy men, who were ages 39 to 59 at the study's outset, were followed for eight to nine years to see which ones would develop the heart condition. About half of the men were rated as showing Type A tendencies when the study began, while the others were rated Type B. The Type A men went

Aggressive actions can be a manifestation of the hard-driving Type A behavior pattern.

on to develop coronary heart disease twice as often as Type B subjects. This increased risk was independent of that conferred by other factors such as smoking.

Alas, science is rarely as simple as that. It soon became clear that Type A was not the end of the trail, but the beginning. A major study of the same magnitude as Friedman and Rosenman's, the Multiple Risk Factor Intervention Trial, failed to replicate their basic findings. Then a pair of carefully controlled studies found that being Type A was associated with better survival rather than worse. One possible explanation: Type As could be just as driven and disciplined about following doctor's orders as they are about work. As researchers tried to sort through this confusion, they came to suspect that some of the original Type A characteristics were irrelevant and thus were muddying the results.

The Hostility-Cardiovascular Disease Link

Over the past few decades, several attempts have been made to refine the original Type A concept. Some of the most influential work has been done by Redford Williams, M.D., a professor of psychiatry and psychology at Duke University in Durham, N.C., who contends that the critical component in Type A behavior is hostility. One noteworthy 1980 study by Williams and his colleagues included 424 patients who underwent a diagnostic procedure for suspected coronary heart disease. The researchers found that those patients who scored high on a questionnaire designed to assess hostility were more likely than others to have severe atherosclerosis, or hardening and narrowing of the coronary artery.

Williams has identified three potentially harmful aspects of *hostility: cynicism,* an attitude of mistrust regarding the motives of other people; *anger,* the emotion often engendered by cynical expectations; and *aggression,* the behavior to which many hostile people resort when they experience angry emotions.

Some of Williams's latest work is aimed at determining whether just watching aggressive behavior is enough to boost a person's risk of heart disease. In a preliminary study, 40 people watched violent movie

Media violence may be hazardous to your health.

scenes while hooked up to heart monitors. The researchers found that viewers had higher blood pressures and heart rates after watching physically violent acts against a victim of the same gender. Watching physical violence against a victim of the opposite sex had no such effect. "This is a crucial distinction, because it indicates that the meaning of the violence was important," says Williams. "Getting a larger blood pressure increase seemed to require that the viewer identify more closely with the person being physically harmed."

The same subjects also had higher levels of three stress hormones in their urine after watching physical violence. Says Williams, "Our findings support the argument that media violence can be hazardous to your health."

C Is for Cancer

Psychologist Lydia Temoshok, Ph.D., has described a third constellation of behaviors that she believes may contribute to cancer progression. What she has called *Type C behavior pattern* includes self-sacrifice, extreme niceness, passive coping, appeasement, and *nonexpression* of emotions—that is, the holding in of emotions, especially anger and other unpleasant feelings. Nonexpression is thought to be the core factor in this cluster of traits. "It seems to be analogous to hostility's role in the Type A behavior pattern," says Temoshok, who is now conducting research on social and behavioral aspects of HIV for the U.S. Department of Defense and the World Health Organization in Geneva.

Temoshok has posited a continuum of coping styles, with Type A and Type C as opposite extremes, while Type B is the healthy middle ground. In the 1980s, Temoshok conducted a series of studies involving patients with malignant melanoma, the deadliest type of skin cancer. These form much of the framework upon which her theory is built.

In one study, Temoshok and her coauthor recruited three groups of subjects: 20 melanoma patients, 20 heart patients, and 20 healthy people. Each subject was shown 50 slides of different anxiety-provoking statements. The person's degree of physiological arousal was measured objectively, and each subject was also asked to rate subjectively how much each statement bothered him or her. A repressive coping style was defined as expressing much less upset than was measured physiologically. As predicted, the cancer patients were more repressed than the other groups.

It Couldn't Have Happened to a Nicer Guy

Temoshok's notion fits the common belief, based on clinical observation, that cancer patients are often "the nicest people." As with the Type A behavior pattern, however, real life has proved to be messier than abstract theory. Several larger studies by other researchers have failed to demonstrate a link between different personality variables and cancer progression.

One of the most widely cited is a 1985 study that appeared in the *New England Journal of Medicine*. It was led by psychologist Barrie Cassileth, Ph.D., of the University of North Carolina in Chapel Hill. In this study, the researchers gave personality tests to

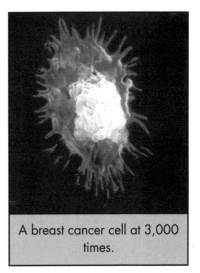

A breast cancer cell at 3,000 times.

two groups of cancer patients: 204 with inoperable advanced tumors, who were studied to determine how long they survived, and 155 with high-risk melanoma or breast cancer, who were studied to determine how long they went without a recurrence.

Cassileth and her colleagues found no relationship between psychological and social factors and the length of survival or the time to relapse. Temoshok has responded that they simply weren't looking at the right factors. For example, there was no measure of emotional expression. In addition, it's conceivable that the outcome of Cassileth's study would have been different had she included cancer patients with more favorable prognoses, who may be more apt to be affected by psychological and social influences. Clearly, more studies are needed to explore the link, if any, between the Type C behavior pattern and cancer progression.

Helpless and Hopeless

A number of other emotions and attitudes have been tied to adverse health effects as well. Prominent among these is *learned helplessness*, a giving-up reaction that follows from the belief that whatever you do doesn't matter. Martin Seligman, Ph.D., a world-renowned psychologist at the University of Pennsylvania, has been at the forefront of this research.

In one well-known experiment, Seligman and his colleagues implanted cancer cells in laboratory rats. The cancer was of a type that is invariably fatal if allowed to grow. However, the number of cells used was such that, under normal circumstances, half of the rats would reject the tumor and live. The next day, some of the rats were given mild escapable shock; some, mild inescapable shock; and some, no shock at all. The researchers found that those rats which had received inescapable shock, and thus were presumed to have learned helplessness, were only half as likely to reject the tumor and twice as likely to die as rats in the other two groups.

It's a big jump from rats to people, and findings in other animals are not necessarily transferable to humans. However, *pessimism* seems to put people at higher risk for illness, too. Seligman believes that the main modulator of learned helplessness in people is *explanatory style,* the manner in which you routinely explain to yourself why things happen. He contends that explanatory style determines how helpless—or how energized—a person becomes when faced with setbacks. Three critical dimensions of explanatory style are *permanence, pervasiveness,* and *personalization.* According to Seligman, pessimistic people tend to believe that the causes of bad events are permanent, while good events have transient causes; that bad events have universal causes, while good events are caused by specific factors; and that bad events are caused by them, while good events are caused by outside forces.

Seligman has tested his ideas in human subjects, too. One 35-year study for which Seligman also served as coauthor was headed by University of Michigan psychology professor Christopher Peterson, Ph.D. The study included 99 men who had been identified as exceptionally gifted members of the Harvard classes of 1942–1944. These men had written essays in 1946 describing their wartime experiences. When these essays were later rated for explanatory style, it turned out that pessimism in early adulthood was linked to poor health at ages 45 through 60.

In its most exaggerated form, pessimism can be virtually indistinguishable from depression. Seligman has documented a number of similarities between the responses of people and animals in his learned-helplessness experiments, on the one hand, and the characteristics of depressed people, on the other. For example, animals given inescapable

Getting to Know You

If you . . .

- explosively accent key words in your everyday speech, even when there is no good reason for such emphasis
- find it almost intolerable to perform boring, repetitive chores such as writing checks or washing dishes
- attempt to fit more and more activities into less and less time, while making fewer and fewer allowances for unforeseen circumstances

. . . then you may have a Type A behavior pattern, according to Friedman and Rosenman (*Type A Behavior and Your Heart*, 1974).

If you . . .

- automatically do a favor when asked by someone you care about, even if you'd rather not
- tend to focus more on a significant other's needs than your own
- try to compose yourself as quickly as possible when getting too emotional

. . . then you may have a Type C coping style, according to Temoshok (*The Type C Connection: The Mind-Body Link to Cancer and Your Health*, 1992).

If you . . .

- habitually check to see if anyone ahead of you in the express line at the supermarket has more items than the limit
- find that having to put up with incompetent people at work really ticks you off
- flash your lights or honk your horn when another driver cuts in front of you

... then you may be prone to hostility, according to Williams (*Anger Kills: Seventeen Strategies for Controlling the Hostility That Can Harm Your Health*, 1993).

If you . . .

- think "the boss is a jerk," rather than "the boss is in a bad mood"
- think "all teachers are unfair," rather than "my math teacher is unfair"
- think "I'm not talented at poker," rather than "I'm not lucky at poker"

... then you may be prone to pessimism, according to Seligman (*Learned Optimism: How to Change Your Mind and Your Life*, 1990).

If you . . .

- can't enjoy things you used to take pleasure in
- don't think of yourself as useful or needed
- feel downhearted and blue in most situations

... then you may be suffering from depression, according to the National Foundation for Depressive Illness.

Depressed people often lose interest in the things they once enjoyed.

shock lose interest in their usual activities—one of the criteria used to diagnose a major depressive episode. In addition, drugs that relieve depression also reduce the symptoms of learned helplessness in animals.

The Depression-Cardiovascular Disease Link

Think of all the ways we describe sadness in our culture: a sad or grieving person is "heartsick" or "downhearted" or "heartbroken." There's mounting evidence that *depression*—the abnormal, persistent version of these normal, transient feelings—may affect survival in people with cardiovascular disease.

Nancy Frasure-Smith, Ph.D., an associate professor of psychiatry at McGill University and a senior research associate at the Montreal Heart Institute, headed up a 1995 study that looked at the impact of depression on the prognosis of heart attack victims. The subjects were 222 patients who had taken part in interviews designed to measure how depressed they were about a week after having a heart attack. Eighteen months later, the patients or their families were contacted again. The researchers found that depression in the hospital following a heart attack was a predictor of death from heart disease over the next year and a half. "The impact was about as great as that of more established risk factors, such as having had a previous heart attack," says Frasure-Smith.

Depression may leave its victims "heartsick" in more ways than one.

A 1993 study by other researchers from the Universities of Maryland and

Iowa and Johns Hopkins University yielded similar results in stroke patients. In that report, patients who were depressed about two weeks after having a stroke were three times more likely to die within the next 10 years.

Social Studies Reports

Hostility, pessimism, and depression are rather unappealing qualities. It stands to reason, then, that people with these traits might find themselves somewhat socially isolated. Some scientists have gone so far as to suggest that isolation itself may account for part of the negative health impact associated with these psychological factors.

A case in point is *bereavement*—the grief that accompanies the death of a loved one—which combines elements of both profound social loss and deep sorrow. Not surprisingly, it seems to have a detrimental effect on the survivor's well-being. For example, in a 1993 study from the Yale University School of Medicine, researchers followed 1,046 married indi-

Social support can improve the odds of staying well and surviving illness.

viduals aged 65 and older for six years. They found that men whose wives died had a higher risk of dying themselves within the first six months after their loss. This risk increase seemed to exceed anything that could be accounted for by the men's prior health status.

Fortunately, the converse also appears to be true: Having plenty of *social support*—that is, a network of supportive contacts with other people—seems to be good for your health. A landmark study that illustrates this point included over 4,700 adults from Alameda County, Calif. Nine years after an initial survey, the researchers, led by epidemiologist Lisa Berkman, Ph.D., now of Harvard University, tracked down what had happened to these people. One thing they looked at was the relationship between death rate and four types of social bonds: marital status, contact with close friends and family, church membership, and other group associations. In each instance, they found that people with social relationships had lower death rates than people with no such ties. Those with the fewest social contacts were twice as likely to have died during the study period as those with the strongest bonds, even when health habits such as smoking and alcohol use were taken into account.

Once you're sick, social involvement still seems to improve the odds of staying alive. A 1992 study by Williams and his colleagues included 1,368 patients with documented atherosclerosis of the coronary artery. These patients had provided information on their social relationships at the time that they underwent a diagnostic procedure at Duke Medical Center. The patients were then contacted annually for several years. The researchers found that people who either were married or had a confidant were three times less likely to die within five years than unmarried people without a close friend in whom they could confide.

Of course, social relationships don't necessarily equal social support. When such contacts are unsupportive, the results may be deleterious. For instance, a new study by Kemeny and others suggests that HIV infection may progress more rapidly in those gay men who are most concerned about social rejection based on their homosexuality.

Paying Religious Attention to Your Health

One type of social involvement that is attracting growing interest is religious participation. Jeff Levin, Ph.D., an associate professor of family

Religious rituals may allay anxiety and depression and promote health.

health and community medicine at Eastern Virginia Medical School, has reviewed this subject at length. "There now have been a few hundred studies that found, in simple terms, a correlation between religious variables and health variables," says Levin. "The question I've asked is, why?"

Levin has proposed a dozen hypotheses that might help explain religion's salutary effect on health. A few are outlined below:

- **Psychosocial effects.** Religion may promote a sense of belonging. By encouraging fellowship, it may provide social support.
- **Belief systems.** The beliefs of certain religious groups may give rise to feelings of peacefulness, self-confidence, and purpose.
- **Religious rites.** Public and private rituals may serve to allay anxiety, reduce hostility, and moderate loneliness and depression.
- **Power of faith.** The certain expectation that particular beliefs or practices will bring rewards may, in itself, lead to healing.
- **Healthy behaviors.** Many religious traditions encourage health-promoting behaviors, such as abstaining from meat or alcohol.

Although Levin continues to explore the link between religion and health, some of his latest work deals with another subject: the health effects of love. "I started to give some thought to what might really be healing about religious involvement. It struck me that love could be underlying all this. Surprisingly, there's a huge literature in medicine and psychology and sociology on all these other constructs, but not much on love. Yet what emotion could be more fundamental than that?"

Learning the Three Cs

If negative psychological traits can be harmful, are positive coping styles helpful? Some of the most highly regarded work in this area has been done by psychologist Suzanne Kobasa, Ph.D., of the City University of New York. The story goes that, when Kobasa was still a graduate student at the University of Chicago, she had a revelation while flipping through a magazine in a waiting room. She came across one of those do-it-yourself stress quizzes, and when she added up her score, she found it put her in the danger zone for becoming ill—yet she was fine. Surely, she thought, some folks are better able than others to deal with the bumps in life.

In the mid-1970s, Kobasa and her colleagues began studying a group of middle managers and top executives at Illinois Bell Telephone. In the process, they identified a hardy personality style that seems to help some people resist the health-eroding effects of stress. Kobasa believes that the "three Cs" of *hardiness* are *commitment, challenge,* and *control.* People who are low in commitment feel alienated, while hardy individuals who are high on this dimension find meaning in their work and personal lives. People low in challenge interpret stressful events as threats, while hardy folks high on this dimension see them as challenges to be met with expected success. People low in control feel powerless in the face of overwhelming forces, while those high on this dimension have a sense of mastery over their circumstances.

In fact, individuals with a strong sense of control over important life events have been shown in numerous studies to be happier and healthier than those who feel relatively helpless. In a classic study coauthored by psychologist Judith Rodin, Ph.D., now president of the University of Pennsylvania, some of the residents in a nursing home were allowed to make decisions about their daily lives, such as whether to watch a movie, while others were not. After three weeks, those given greater control were more content and active. Eighteen months later, only 15 percent of those in the enhanced control group had died, compared to 30 percent of the other group.

More recently, George Solomon, M.D., a professor of psychiatry and biobehavioral sciences at the University of California in Los Angeles, headed up a study of HIV-positive patients who are long-term survivors. The researchers found that the patients' immunity was consistently boosted by one quality: *assertiveness,* the ability to take confident action. Solomon reported that those patients with a stronger drive survived longer with the virus than their more passive counterparts. Specifically, having a strong sense of self-worth, being able to say "no" when appropriate, and being willing to demand what they wanted were characteristics often seen in the survivors.

Don't Worry, Be Healthy

Of course, take-charge people get sick, too. To say that positive thinking is all that's needed to keep from developing cancer or progressing to full-blown AIDS would be a gross oversimplification of these researchers' ideas. The fact is, no one really knows all the variables that are involved in disease development and progression, but they're undoubtedly multiple and complex.

Simplistic overreliance on positive thinking can backfire badly, if it causes people to become depressed because they blame themselves for causing their own disease or if it isolates people by pressuring them to conform to someone else's idea of how they ought to feel. The most that can be said is that certain traits such as optimism and assertiveness may be beneficial as a general rule in certain circumstances, while other traits such as depression and hostility may be harmful. If becoming more upbeat and self-assertive also makes you happier, then you've probably got nothing to lose.

Happiness, in turn, may lead to healthiness, although there are no guarantees. However, an interesting finding in this respect was presented at the 1995 meeting of the American Psychosomatic Society. In a preliminary study from the Institute of HeartMath, a private research and education organization in Boulder Creek, Calif., merely thinking appreciative thoughts caused the parasympathetic nervous system, which helps protect the heart, to become more active. It seems that just taking time to smell the roses—or plant the cactus, if that's what gives you pleasure—may do your heart good in more ways than one.

Minding the Body:
Psychoneuro-immunology

Mind moves matter.
Virgil

Intelligence is in every cell of your body. The mind is not confined to the space above the neck.
Candace Pert, Ph.D.

I t is not every year that a new field of science is named. That's exactly what happened in 1981, though, when Robert Ader, Ph.D., published a book he had edited under the title *Psychoneuroimmunology.* The unwieldy name stuck. Thus, Ader christened a new discipline, since nicknamed PNI, that has become one of the hottest areas of scientific research and debate.

This burgeoning field of PNI is concerned with exploring how the immune system and the brain interact to influence health. Just as Western philosophy for centuries separated body and mind, Western medicine in earlier decades held that the immune system acts independently of the rest of the body. More recently, however, scientists have begun to recognize links between the immune system, which defends the body against foreign invaders; the endocrine system, which secretes powerful hormones; and the nervous system, which includes the brain. The immune system may be a star defensive player, but it's still just part of a team.

Of Mice and Men

The ideas underlying PNI are now widely accepted. However, in 1974, they were still radical notions capable of sending shock waves through the scientific community. That's when Ader, a psychologist at the University of Rochester in New York, made what ultimately proved to be a breakthrough discovery. He was conducting a classical conditioning experiment with rats, similar to the type Russian researcher Ivan Pavlov had made famous with dogs. In Ader's experiment, he was trying to teach the rats to associate nausea with the taste of saccharin-sweetened water, which is harmless by itself. He did this by pairing the sweetened water with injections of the drug cyclophosphamide, which causes nausea, on the first day of the study. On subsequent days, he offered the rats sweetened water without the drug and recorded how much they drank, as a measure of how long they "remembered" the nausea association.

Then Ader hit a snag. After several days, some of the rats, although young and healthy, began to sicken and die. Ader knew that cyclophosphamide, the nausea-inducing drug, is also a powerful suppressant of the immune system. He realized that the rats had come to associate not only nausea, but also immune suppression with the sweetened water. With each drink, the rats had "believed" they were getting more of the drug, and their immune systems had responded accordingly. This, in turn, had left them more susceptible to disease. It was a startling revelation, because, up until that time, medical wisdom had held that the brain and immune system are completely autonomous entities, unable to affect each other this way. Ader soon joined with University of Rochester immunologist Nicholas Cohen, Ph.D., to further explore behaviorally conditioned immune suppression. The pair's elegant experiments are credited with putting PNI on the map.

Several years later, Ader teamed up with Karen Olness, M.D., a pediatrician at Case Western Reserve University in Cleveland, to test the same approach in a human. The patient in question was a 13-year-old girl called Marette, who suffered from severe lupus, an autoimmune disease that can damage the skin, kidneys, blood vessels, nervous system, heart, and other internal organs. Despite treatment, Marette's disease had progressed to a life-threatening stage. In a last-ditch effort to suppress the girl's self-destructive immune reactions, her doctors wanted to try cyclophosphamide—the same drug Ader had used in his rat experiment. There was a catch, however: the drug was known to be toxic. Therefore, to limit the dose and reduce the risk, they decided to also try conditioning.

The doctors wanted to pair administration of the drug with a truly

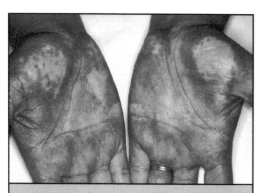

A person with systemic lupus erythematosus (SLE) usually develops a skin rash along with other symptoms.

unforgettable taste, so they gave Marette cod liver oil along with her injections. At the same time, they also gave her a whiff of rose perfume, because they weren't sure whether Marette was more likely to be conditioned by taste or smell. After three initial pairings, the doctors began to alternate such drug treatments with treatments in which the taste and smell were presented alone, without any medication actually being given. Over 6 months' time, the girl received six rather than 12 drug treatments. Yet she continued to do as well as might be expected on a full-dose regimen. Unfortunately, after a year, she became so nauseated by the sight of cod liver oil that she could no longer swallow it, but by then her illness was stabilized. Although no firm conclusions can be drawn from an individual case such as Marette's, the results are certainly intriguing.

Speaking to the Immune System

Once scientists accepted that the nervous and immune systems interact, they began to look for physical connections. A pivotal discovery, made in the early 1980s, was that organs of the immune system are richly endowed with nerves. David Felten, M.D., Ph.D., a professor of neurobiology and anatomy and a pioneer in this work, has recalled that he was viewing sections of spleen under a microscope when he realized that he was looking at nerve fibers—fibers that, according to prevailing thought, shouldn't have been there. Since that time, Felten and his colleagues at the University of Rochester—including his wife and research partner, Suzanne Felten, Ph.D.—have used fluorescent dyes to trace nerve pathways to such lymphoid organs as the thymus and lymph nodes.

Soldiers in the Defending Army

The immune system consists of a complex network of cells and organs that are specially adapted to defend the body against attack by outside forces. When all goes according to plan, these immune defenses are directed against disease-causing agents, such as viruses, bacteria, and fungi.

However, when things go awry, the immune system can mistake a normally harmless substance, such as pollen or dust, for a threat, causing an allergy. Or the immune system can turn its weapons against the body itself, producing so-called *autoimmune diseases*, such as rheumatoid arthritis and systemic lupus erythematosus. When the immune system is missing one or more key components, the result is an *immunodeficiency disorder*, such as AIDS. The immune system also plays a critical role in fighting off cancer. One theory states that immune cells patrol the body, seeking out and killing off any cancerous cells there. Tumors develop when this surveillance and defense system breaks down or becomes overwhelmed.

The various specialized cells of the immune system comprise a formidable army. Among the types of immune cells are:

- *Lymphocytes.* These small white blood cells, numbering about one trillion, carry out the most important work of the immune system. There are two main kinds of lymphocytes: B cells and T cells.
- *B cells.* These lymphocytes work chiefly by secreting *antibodies*, tiny proteins that ambush any bacteria, viruses, and other foreign invaders, known as *antigens*, that are circulating in the bloodstream. Each B cell produces one kind of antibody, which fights a single type of antigen.
- *T cells.* These lymphocytes work primarily by secreting

Computer graphic image of a T cell. These white blood cells play an important role in the human immune system.

lymphokines, powerful chemical messengers that can mobilize other cells and substances. Cytotoxic, or killer, T cells interact directly with specific targets. They attack body cells that are infected or malignant—or, less helpfully, foreign cells in an organ transplant. Regulatory T cells direct and regulate immune responses. Two kinds of regulatory T cells are helper and suppressor cells.

- *Helper T cells.* These T cells stimulate B cells to produce antibodies. They also activate cytotoxic T cells and initiate other immune responses. A disastrous decline in the number of helper T cells is characteristic of AIDS.
- *Suppressor T cells.* These T cells turn off helper T cells when enough antibodies have been produced. They also shut down other immune responses.
- *Natural killer cells.* These lymphocytes, like cytotoxic T cells, are armed with potent chemical weapons. However, they differ from cytotoxic T cells in that they don't have to recognize a specific antigen before launching an all-out attack. Instead, they can target a wide range of enemies.
- *Phagocytes.* These "cell eaters" are large white cells that can swallow and digest microbes and other foreign particles. Phagocytes called *monocytes* develop into macrophages when they enter tissues.
- *Macrophages.* These "big eater" phagocytes are versatile cells that devour microbes and "present" antigens to helper T cells.

The organs of the immune system are known as *lymphoid organs,* because they are where lymphocytes develop and congregate. These include the bone marrow, thymus, lymph nodes, spleen, tonsils and adenoids, appendix, and clumps of lymphoid tissue in the small intestine. In addition, the lymphatic and blood vessels that carry lymphocytes are sometimes considered lymphoid organs.

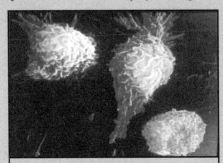

Macrophages—the largest white blood cells.

Anatomical links are only part of the picture, however. The intricate two-way communication process between the nervous, endocrine, and immune systems also depends on a variety of biochemical messengers. In 1973, Candace Pert, Ph.D., while still a graduate student at Johns Hopkins University in Baltimore, made a revolutionary discovery: Working with eminent neuroscientist Solomon

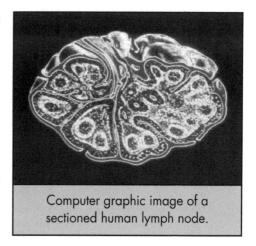

Computer graphic image of a sectioned human lymph node.

Snyder, M.D., she found that opiate drugs such as morphine can bind to cells in the brain. Since there was no reason for the brain to have special receptors for these drugs, the implication was that the body must make its own morphinelike chemicals.

Two years later, the first of the body's natural opiates was identified. This group of chemicals was dubbed *endorphins*, from *endo*genous, meaning inside the organism, and m*orphines*. Like other opiates, they block pain and induce euphoric feelings, including the "runner's high." Endorphins are part of a larger class of chemicals called *neuropeptides*, strings of amino acids released by nerve cells. Neuropeptides, which have effects that often mimic those of mood-altering drugs, are present in high concentrations in the *limbic system*, part of the brain that is the main control center for emotions and drives. This led Pert, today a Rutgers neuroscientist, to propose that neuropeptides and their receptors might be nothing less than "the biochemical correlates of emotions."

About 60 different neuropeptides have now been identified. Pert and other researchers soon began searching for neuropeptides and their receptors not only in the brain, but throughout the body. Scientists found them, among other places, in the gastrointestinal tract—giving new meaning to the term "gut feelings." More interestingly, researchers found them on all the primary cells of the immune system. For example, Pert and her colleagues discovered that a whole range of neuropeptides, from opiates to Valium-like chemicals, can latch onto germ-eating immune cells called macrophages and influence the speed or direction of their movement. In theory, then, neuropeptides might be tangible links between the emotions and the way the body fights disease.

While emotion is important, so is intellect. French immunologist Gérard Renoux carried the search for mind-body connections to the *cerebral cortex,* the thin, enfolded outer layer of the brain that in humans is regarded as the seat of reason, language, and perception. Renoux and his colleagues found that destroying part of a mouse's cortex, which didn't significantly alter the animal's behavior, did change its immune function. The specific nature of the effect depended upon which side of the cortex was damaged, with the two sides seeming to work together in a delicate balance.

Talking Back to the Brain

Neuropeptides aren't the only chemicals that "speak" to the immune system. *Hormones,* substances released mainly by endocrine glands that help regulate body activities, do so as well. *Corticosteroid* hormones, for example, which are released by the adrenal glands in response to stress signals, have been shown to decrease antibodies and reduce lymphocytes in both number and strength.

Moreover, the body's communication lines flow two ways, allowing the immune system to "talk" back to the brain. In the 1970s, Argentine-born Hugo Besedovsky, a doctor at the Swiss Research Institute, began looking for signs of this connection, which logic told him must be there. He and his colleagues implanted electrodes in the brains of rats, then injected the animals with foreign cells to rouse their immune systems into action. The researchers found that, as this was happening, electrical activity in the rat's brain rose and levels of certain brain chemicals temporarily fell. Thus, Besedovsky's ground-breaking work supplied the first firm evidence that the brain knew something about what the immune system was doing.

Starting in 1979, microbiologist Edwin Blalock, Ph.D., of the University of Texas Medical Branch in Galveston, demonstrated that immune cells can not only understand, but also speak the language of hormones. Blalock was studying *interferons,* chemicals released by white blood cells that help fight off viruses, when he noticed something unexpected: *ACTH* (short for adrenocorticotropic hormone), a hormone secreted by the pituitary gland, kept turning up in a laboratory flask filled only with human immune cells.

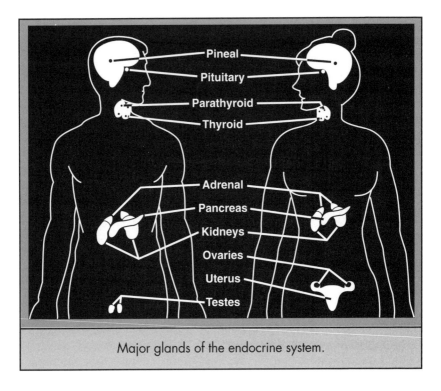

Major glands of the endocrine system.

Before long, Blalock had reached the surprising conclusion that immune cells were making hormones in addition to interferons. Not only that, but depending upon conditions, they could make a whole array of such chemicals: ACTH, growth hormone, thyroid-stimulating hormone, reproductive hormones, and endorphins. Blalock has speculated that the immune system may function as a "sixth sense," telling the brain about invaders and helping regulate the body's response.

PNI: Pretty Nifty Insights

PNI can be defined as the study of interactions among behavior (*psycho*), neural and endocrine function (*neuro*), and immune processes (*immunology*). Some other provocative lines of PNI research include:

- **Brain lesions and the immune system.** Lesions in the brain's hypothalamus reduce the production of antibodies, while stimulation in the same area can enhance antibody production.
- **Hormone receptors on immune cells.** Scientists have found receptors on lymphocytes for such hormones as corticosteroids, insulin, testosterone, estrogens, and growth hormone.
- **Lymphokines and the pituitary gland.** *Interleukin-1,* a lymphokine released by monocytes and macrophages, stimulates pituitary cells to produce hormones such as ACTH.
- **Cell types common to both systems.** Cells containing *chromogranin,* a chemical of the neuroendocrine system, are also found in the spleen, thymus, and lymph nodes.
- **Chemicals common to both systems.** *Neuroleukin,* a substance that promotes the survival of certain nerve cells, is also a lymphokine product that may induce B cell maturation.
- **Neural effects of immune stimulants.** *Mitogens,* powerful nonspecific immune stimulants that cause lymphocyte multiplication, bind to certain nerve cells and alter their activity.
- **Lymphokine production by neural cells.** Purified and enriched cultures of certain glia cells of the central nervous system are able to secrete interleukin-1 when stimulated.
- **Brain dominance and immune disease.** Left-handers, whose brain functions are atypically distributed between the two sides of the brain, are prone to autoimmune diseases.

A particularly promising area of PNI research explores the body's stress response and its implications for a wide range of diseases.

The Brain-Arthritis Link

Lupus and rheumatoid arthritis are two examples of autoimmune diseases that involve inflammation. Anyone with rheumatoid arthritis can tell you about the redness, warmth, swelling, pain, and loss of function that can accompany joint inflammation. What the person may not know, however, is the complexity of what's going on inside the body. Redness and warmth, for instance, result when lymphokines and other substances cause small blood vessels in the area to become dilated and carry more blood. Swelling occurs when other immune secretions make the vessels leaky, allowing fluid and immune substances to seep into surrounding tissue and immune cells to converge on the site.

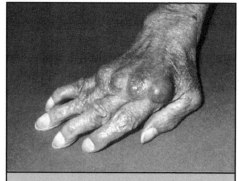

Inflammation is the body's natural response to injury. But what causes the overactive inflammatory response in a condition such as rheumatoid arthritis? One leading researcher who is trying to answer that question is Esther Sternberg, M.D., chief of the National Institute of Mental Health's Section on Neuroendocrine Immunology and Behavior. "We are studying the role of the brain and the central nervous system in susceptibility to inflammatory disease," she says. Much of her work is done in two strains of rat, one of which is highly susceptible to inflammatory disease, and the other of which is resistant. When researchers expose the susceptible rats to certain bacterial cell walls, the animals develop a type of arthritis that closely resembles human rheumatoid arthritis. In contrast, the resistant rats tend to remain unaffected by the same stimuli.

In a person with rheumatoid arthritis, the immune system turns its weapons against the body itself.

"What happens under normal circumstances is that, as soon as an organism encounters something in the environment that causes inflammation, the immune system is turned on," explains Sternberg. "The immune cells send signals to the brain, which starts up the body's stress response. And the end result of this is that the adrenal glands secrete corticosteroids, which have an anti-inflammatory effect. They shut off the inflammation that began the process in the first place." In Lewis rats, the strain susceptible to inflammatory disease, the stress response is blunted. However, in Fischer rats, the resistant strain, the stress response swings into vigorous action when confronted with inflammatory stimuli.

"Of course, the story is always more complicated in humans," says Sternberg. "But the studies that we and others are now doing show that people who suffer from various inflammatory diseases do have a blunted stress response, much like the Lewis rats."

The Good, the Bad, and the Ugh

The body's stress response can be helpful; for instance, when it keeps inflammation from spinning out of control, as it does in rheumatoid arthritis. In many cases, however, the effect of stress is far from benign. Among the top scientists studying the role of stress in suppressing the immune system are the husband-wife research team of Ronald Glaser, Ph.D., and Janice Kiecolt-Glaser, Ph.D.

At Ohio State University, Glaser, an immunologist, and Kiecolt-Glaser, a psychologist, have pooled their talents in a series of studies looking at the immune effects of commonplace events. In their first study, they and their colleagues drew blood from 75 medical students on two occasions: first, about a month before final exams, and second, on the initial day of the exam period. The researchers found a decrease in natural killer cell activity in the second sample, indicating that the stress

In medical students, the stress of taking exams can weaken certain key immune system defenses.

caused by taking tests had weakened a key defense. The finding was all the more striking because "these were people who got into medical school by taking exams, so this was a relatively small and very predictable stress for them," says Kiecolt-Glaser.

Exams are a short-term source of stress, but in their current work, the Glasers are focusing on a longer-term problem: the chronic stress that goes along with being the caregiving spouse of an Alzheimer's disease victim. In the first year of an ongoing study, 69 caregivers were matched with an equal number of control subjects similar in age, education, and income. Over a 13-month period, the caregivers showed deterioration relative to the controls on three measures of immune status. In addition, the caregivers reported more days of infectious illness.

The latest data indicate that the caregivers also respond less well to vaccines than the controls, further evidence of their comparatively poor immune function, since vaccines work by provoking an immune response. Even worse, says Kiecolt-Glaser, "older people may not get over chronic stress. Immunologically, we don't see recovery, even an average of two years after the death of the Alzheimer's patient."

The Brain-Common Cold Link

Granted, many kinds of stressors have now been linked to numerous types of immune changes. In most studies, the unanswered question remains: Are those changes great enough to actually affect a person's health? Another researcher who has attempted to address that issue head-on is Sheldon Cohen, Ph.D., a psychology professor at Carnegie Mellon University in Pittsburgh.

In a 1991 study that appeared in the *New England Journal of Medicine,* Cohen and his colleagues asked whether stress would suppress resistance to the common cold. The subjects were 420 healthy adults, who first com-

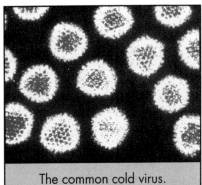

The common cold virus.

pleted questionnaires that assessed how stressful their lives were. Then 394 of the volunteers were given nose drops containing one of five cold viruses, while 26 were given harmless saline nose drops. For the next week, the subjects were quarantined in apartments. During this time, each volunteer was examined daily by a doctor for signs of a cold. The number of facial tissues used by each subject was also counted.

The volunteers were classified as having clinical colds only if they had both a doctor's diagnosis of a cold and laboratory confirmation of infection. Overall, 38 percent of those who had received a virus fell into this category. However, the higher a subject scored on the stress index, the greater the likelihood that he or she would develop a clinical cold. This finding held up even when the researchers took into account health factors that can be affected by stress, including smoking, alcohol consumption, exercise, diet, and quality of sleep.

"There's a large literature showing that stress is related to what psychologists call illness behaviors, and there's also solid evidence that stress and other psychological factors change the immune system," says Cohen. "What hasn't been clear is the extent to which those changes, which tend to be within normal ranges, have implications for disease outcomes. Until recently, the notion that stress influences susceptibility to infectious disease has had very little empirical support."

The Importance of Significance

Cohen's comment raises one of the central issues in psychoneuroimmunology: the relevance of all those esoteric immune measures. When researchers say they've found a significant difference in some variable, they generally mean that the change they've shown is *statistically significant*—in other words, that there's only a small statistical probability that the observed result could have occurred by chance if there really was no effect. However, just because something is statistically significant doesn't necessarily mean it's *clinically significant*—in other words, a meaningful marker for disease. It's quite possible that an immune measure could change in ways that would have few if any practical ramifications for a person's health.

Those markers of immune function that are easiest to measure are not necessarily the ones that are most appropriate. Deciding how to design and interpret a PNI experiment, then, can be a challenge—one that is made all the more difficult by the interdisciplinary nature of the field. It's not easy for a single researcher to master all the disciplines PNI encompasses, just as it's not always easy for scientists from different areas of expertise to collaborate with each other.

Thanks to the recent establishment of specialized training programs in PNI, however, the next generation of scientists may be better equipped to meet these challenges. A number of well-known universities around the United States now offer pre- and postdoctoral training in PNI. Among them are Emory University in Atlanta, Louisiana State University, Ohio State University, the Medical College of Pennsylvania, the University of California in Los Angeles, the University of Colorado in Boulder, the University of Miami, the University of North Carolina in Chapel Hill, the University of Pittsburgh, and the University of Rochester.

In addition, organizations such as the Fetzer Institute in Kalamazoo, Mich., provide support to researchers, educators, journalists, and others who are involved in PNI work. Among other things, the Fetzer Institute publishes *Advances: The Journal of Mind-Body Health* and produced *Healing and the Mind with Bill Moyers,* a five-part PBS television series first aired in February 1993. A sign of the broad public interest this series generated is the fact that 52 TV stations helped set up study groups to discuss mind-body issues after the second airing.

Poems in Body Language

Neuropeptides and hormones "speak" to the immune system. The immune system "talks" back in a language the brain can understand. This "conversation" seems to have something to say about the state of our health.

Throughout this chapter, the two-way communication that exists among body systems has often been described in terms of a "language." It is a readily grasped and remarkably apt metaphor. The basic analogy between grammar and immunology was perhaps best stated by Danish scientist Niels Jerne in a lecture he gave in Stockholm in 1984, when he accepted the Nobel Prize in Medicine—an honor he shared with two other scientists for advances in immunology.

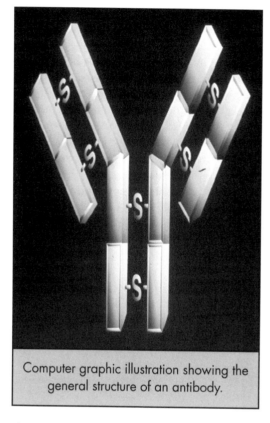

Computer graphic illustration showing the general structure of an antibody.

Jerne noted that all human languages make do with a vocabulary of about a hundred thousand words or less—vocabularies a hundred times smaller than estimates of the size of the antibody repertoire of the immune system. He suggested, then, that the vocabulary of the immune system might be thought of as being composed not of "words," but of "sentences," each of which is "capable of responding to any sentence expressed by the multitude of antigens which the immune system may encounter." So, in Jerne's view, the immune system and brain share yet another characteristic: the innate ability to express themselves in endlessly creative ways.

Of Frontiers and Pioneers

Scientific creativity is reflected in the sudden explosion of mind-body research. A search of the worldwide medical literature under the subject word "psychoneuroimmunology" on MEDLINE, the premier database of the National Library of Medicine, turned up 161 listings for 1992 through the first half of 1995. (Of course, there were many, many other research papers on PNI-related topics listed under narrower subject words.) The same search turned up only four listings for the years 1980 through 1984, evidence of both the field's newness and its growth.

Today PNI research has broadened its reach to include some of the most fascinating subjects in science. At a 1995 conference on PNI, for example, the topics included the influence of patient-health care provider interactions, psychological influences on health, the evidence regarding personality and cancer, mediators of mind-immune interactions, strategies for overcoming the ill effects of stress, psychological interventions in disease, and applications of such interventions to cancer and AIDS. These are among the cutting-edge topics we'll explore in this book as well.

Stress and Dis-stress:
The Relaxation Response

PERTH, SCOTLAND, February 1995—Prisoners at a maximum security jail who are deemed suicide risks are being housed in pastel-painted cells "in a bid to cut stress," reported the PA News wire service. Following a year in which five inmates took their own lives, authorities decided that, in addition to taking ordinary precautions such as removing hazardous objects, they would provide pale pink cells for depressed prisoners.

STOCKHOLM, SWEDEN, February 1995—Swedish bus drivers are being paid "to get rid of their stress by meditating" instead of taking it out on innocent passengers or other drivers, reported the Reuters wire service. According to the local traffic chief, a 40-hour course designed to ease the strain of city driving was offered after many bus drivers complained of "stress-induced" headaches, stomach aches, and stiff muscles.

I n Japan, they say that *karoshi*—death from overwork—claims 30,000 lives each year. In the United States, the consensus seems to be that life has never been more stressful, and work is certainly a major contributor. In the 1991 book *The Overworked American: The Unexpected Decline of Leisure*, a Harvard economist, J. B. Schor, calculated that the average American worker now spends a month longer on the job each year than did folks of the previous generation. Meanwhile, the time spent at paid jobs is almost equaled by the number of hours devoted to unpaid chores, such as housework and child care. Not surprisingly, then, Schor found that the amount of leisure time the typical American has each year has fallen by 47 hours within the last generation.

It's no wonder that being "stressed out" is the mark of modern life—and the bane of modern health. According to the American Institute of

Traffic gridlock—the quintessential symbol of the kinds of stressors encountered in modern life.

Stress, 75 to 90 percent of all visits to physicians are made for stress-related disorders, ranging from heart attacks to some viral infections. Yet such figures are ambiguous, in part because of ambiguity in the definition of stress itself. In fact, scientists at a major conference in 1986 reached the conclusion that no absolute definition of stress is possible. However, in scientific terms, *stress* is not what happens to a person—such outside forces are called *stressors*—but how that person reacts inside to whatever happens.

When different people are exposed to the same stressor, they may respond very differently. Certain individuals, sometimes dubbed *hot reactors*, tend to react excessively to moderate stressors. However, even among other people, stress lies less in an event itself than in a person's perception of it. For example, petting a golden retriever may be relaxing for most of us, but for someone who is deathly afraid of dogs, the same experience would undoubtedly provoke a strong stress response.

That Voodoo That You Do

One dramatic example of the effect of cultural beliefs on the reaction to a stressor is the phenomenon sometimes called *voodoo death*, in which death is apparently brought on by a spell or sorcery. As far back as the sixteenth century, European explorers reported instances of death among American Indians who had been sentenced to die by "medicine men." The fascination with such practices continues today. The 1995 meeting of the American Psychiatric Association, for example, featured a workshop titled Voodoo As It Relates to Medicine Among Haitians.

In a review article first published in 1942, the eminent American physiologist Walter Cannon, M.D., Sc.D., collected several such tales of seem-

Death by voodoo is an extreme example of the dire consequences brought about by severe emotional distress.

ingly mysterious sudden death, which he attributed to "shocking emotional stress." In one case, first recorded a century earlier, a Maori woman in New Zealand ate some fruit and only later learned that it had come from a taboo place. She exclaimed that the chief had been profaned and that his spirit would surely kill her. By noon the next day, the woman was dead. The skeptic might wonder whether fruit from that spot had become taboo precisely because it was unsafe for human consumption. Nevertheless, recent research has shown that extreme emotional distress may indeed trigger some cases of fatal heart attack.

Fright, Fight, and Flight

Cannon is considered a founder of the field of stress physiology. As far back as the mid-1800s, renowned French physiologist Claude Bernard had spoken of something he called the *milieu intérieur,* or inner environment of an organism, which he claimed was essential to understanding disease.

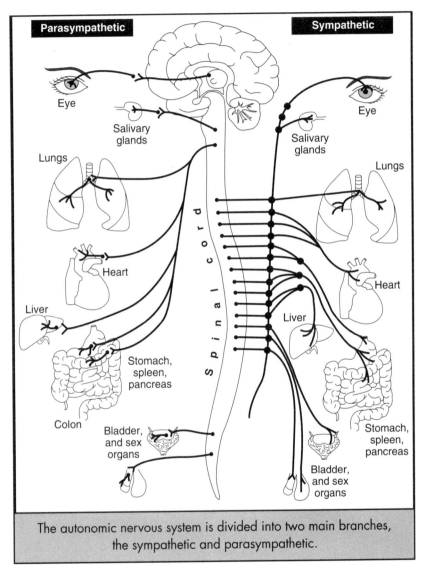

Parasympathetic

Eye

Salivary glands

Lungs

Heart

Liver

Stomach, spleen, pancreas

Colon

Bladder, and sex organs

Sympathetic

Eye

Salivary glands

Lungs

Heart

Liver

Stomach, spleen, pancreas

Bladder, and sex organs

Spinal cord

The autonomic nervous system is divided into two main branches, the sympathetic and parasympathetic.

Cannon further developed this idea in the concept of *homeostasis*, which he described in his classic book *The Wisdom of the Body* as the organism's continual attempt to achieve internal balance in response to external change.

It was Cannon who first outlined the *fight-or-flight response,* the body's internal adaptive response to danger. This fight-or-flight mechanism was essential to survival in the days when humans were faced primarily with acute physical stressors, such as wild animals—the kinds of immediate threats that can be handled effectively by fighting back or running away. In the modern world, however, humans are more often confronted by chronic psychological and social stressors, such as job hassles—the kinds of long-term problems for which this response system is less useful.

Cannon traced the inner workings of stress to the *autonomic nervous system,* that part of the nervous system which is concerned with control of involuntary body functions. There are two major divisions of the autonomic nervous system: the *sympathetic nervous system,* the part that is activated during stress, and the *parasympathetic nervous system,* the part that plays an opposing role.

When things get alarming or exciting, the sympathetic nervous system switches on. The body releases stress hormones called *catecholamines* that arouse key organs. These hormones include *epinephrine* (also called adrenaline) and *norepinephrine* (also called noradrenaline), which take action within seconds. Physiological changes ready the body to meet an emergency. You've surely noticed that your heartbeat and breathing come faster when you're startled. In addition, blood pressure and muscle tension increase sharply, and blood sugar levels rise for quick energy. Cognition is sharpened, and pain perception is dulled. Meanwhile, less urgent activities are deferred. The stomach and small intestine become inactive, and growth and reproductive processes are inhibited.

Rats and the Rat Race

Cannon was the first to recognize the role of the sympathetic nervous system, epinephrine, and norepinephrine in the body's stress response. However, it was left to a clumsy young scientist to make the next step toward formalizing the concept of stress.

In the 1930s, Hans Selye, M.D., Ph.D., who went on to become a world-famous endocrinologist at the University of Montreal and McGill University, was just beginning his career. For an experiment designed to test the effects of a chemical extract, he was injecting rats daily—but not, apparently, without a considerable amount of awkward fumbling, dropping, chasing, and the like. At the end of the study period, Selye exam-

50 Signs You May Be Stressed Out

Following is a list of common signs and symptoms of stress, courtesy of Paul Rosch, M.D., president of the American Institute of Stress:

- Frequent headaches
- Teeth grinding, jaw clenching
- Stuttering, stammering
- Trembling of lips or hands
- Neck stiffness, back pain
- Faintness, dizziness
- Ringing or buzzing sounds
- Frequent blushing or sweating
- Clammy hands or feet
- Difficulty swallowing
- Frequent colds or infections
- Rashes, itching, hives
- Unexplained "allergy" attacks
- Heartburn, stomach pain, nausea
- Excessive belching or flatulence
- Constipation, diarrhea
- Difficulty breathing
- Sudden, severe panic attacks
- Chest pain, palpitations
- Frequent urination
- Decreased sexual desire
- Extreme anxiety or guilt
- Increased anger or frustration
- Depression, wild mood swings
- Increased or decreased appetite
- Insomnia, nightmares
- Difficulty concentrating
- Trouble learning new material
- Forgetfulness, confusion

- Difficulty making decisions
- Feeling overwhelmed
- Frequent crying spells
- Feeling lonely or worthless
- Little interest in appearance
- Fidgeting, foot tapping
- Increased irritability
- Overreacting to petty hassles
- Frequent minor accidents
- Obsessive or compulsive behavior
- Reduced work efficiency
- Excuses to cover up poor work
- Rapid or mumbled speech
- Extreme defensiveness
- Trouble communicating
- Social withdrawal and isolation
- Constant fatigue or weakness
- Habitual nonprescription drug use
- Unintentional weight gain or loss
- Increased smoking or drinking
- Excessive gambling or spending

Keep in mind that the above symptoms may have other causes besides stress. Check with your physician for an individual evaluation.

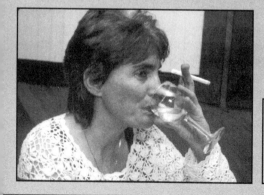

Increased smoking or drinking is often associated with severe stress.

ined the rats and found that their physical condition had indeed changed. They'd developed peptic ulcers, enlarged adrenal glands, and shrunken immune tissues. There was just one catch: rats in a control group, injected daily with saline solution, had developed identical changes. When Selye considered what the two groups might have in common, he realized it could be the traumatic injections.

To test his idea that the animals were showing a generalized response to unpleasantness, Selye tried subjecting other groups of rats to different unpleasant experiences, such as cold, heat, and forced exercise. In all cases, he found the same kinds of changes. He concluded that what the rats were undergoing was a nonspecific stress response that he termed the *general adaptation syndrome.*

If Cannon is the grandfather of modern stress research, Selye is the father. He was among the first to show that emotional upset can lead to physical disease through chemical mind-body links. However, he also made it clear that not all states of stress are noxious. Selye believed that mild, brief, and controllable episodes of stress—what he called "the salt of life"—could actually be perceived as pleasant or exciting and could prompt positive emotional and intellectual growth. It was only the more severe, protracted, and uncontrollable situations of distress that he believed led to disease.

Selye also pioneered the study of *glucocorticoids,* another class of hormones released as part of the stress response. Glucocorticoids, which often behave similarly to epinephrine, are among the corticosteroid hormones secreted by the adrenal glands. While epinephrine acts within seconds, glucocorticoids maintain this activity over minutes or hours. Taken together, epinephrine, norepinephrine, and the glucocorticoids are responsible for much of what happens within the body during stress.

It's now recognized that ultimate control over glucocorticoid secretion lies with the brain. It works like this: The brain senses or anticipates a stressor, and the *hypothalamus,* the base of the brain, releases the hormone CRF (short for *corticotropin releasing factor*). CRF travels through a special circulatory system to the *pituitary gland,* connected to the hypothalamus by a short stalk. At the pituitary, CRF triggers the release of the hormone ACTH (adrenocorticotropic hormone) into the bloodstream. When ACTH reaches the *adrenal glands,* located on top of the kidneys, it causes the release of glucocorticoids.

Life Is a Long Emergency

For someone who is under constant deadline pressure or beaten down by financial burdens, life today can seem like one long emergency. We now know that long-term activation of the stress response can damage the health in numerous ways. Over time, the associated cardiovascular changes can promote high blood pressure, which, in turn, may contribute to heart attack, stroke, kidney failure, and atherosclerosis (a form of hardening of the arteries). The increased muscle tension can lead to headaches, and changes in the activity of the digestive tract can result in diarrhea or stomach pain.

In addition, when blood sugar is constantly mobilized instead of stored, healthy tissues can atrophy, and fatigue may occur. When constructive body processes are indefinitely put on hold, immune function

Like humans, free-ranging olive baboons in Kenya are subject to a variety of social stressors.

may be blunted, tissue repair and growth may be impaired, and fertility may be reduced.

An unusual approach to exploring the effects of stress has been taken by Robert Sapolsky, Ph.D., a professor of biological sciences and neuroscience at Stanford University: studying stress among free-living olive baboons in Kenya. Sapolsky has written that these intelligent, social animals are good stand-ins for human subjects in stress research because, as is the case with people, their main stressors are psychological rather than physical. In other words, since the olive baboons food is plentiful and their predators are few, the animals have lots of time to distress each other, just as humans do. Sapolsky found that male baboons tended to respond very differently to potential stressors depending on their social rank in a troop, with subordinate males showing hormonal and physiological changes that were more likely to set them up for stress-related disease. Interestingly, these were also the baboons who, compared to the dominant males, had lower degrees of social control, less frequent social contacts, and fewer outlets for their frustration—some of the same kinds of factors thought to predispose humans to develop stress-related illness, too.

The exact way stress affects a particular person may be due, in part, to an inborn vulnerability. A case in point is asthma. David Mrazek, M.D., chairman of psychiatry at Children's National Medical Center in Washington, D.C., is investigating the possible role of stress in determining which genetically predisposed infants actually go on to develop asthma. In a 1994 study, Mrazek and his colleagues followed 150 children of mothers with asthma for the first three years of life. When each child was three weeks old, a researcher paid a home visit to observe the mother and child together. The mothers were also interviewed to learn more about any difficulties they might be having caring for their babies or coping with work and family demands. Of those children who developed asthma by age three, 64 percent had mothers with some parenting problems, compared to 36 percent of children who remained asthma-free.

The Stress-Hypertension Link

Clearly, not everyone is equally prone to the harmful health effects of stress. A leading figure in the study of racial differences in susceptibility to hypertension, or high blood pressure, is Joel Dimsdale, M.D., a psychiatry professor at the University of California in San Diego and editor-in-chief of the journal *Psychosomatic Medicine*.

According to the American Heart Association, blacks in the United States are twice as likely as whites to have moderate high blood pressure

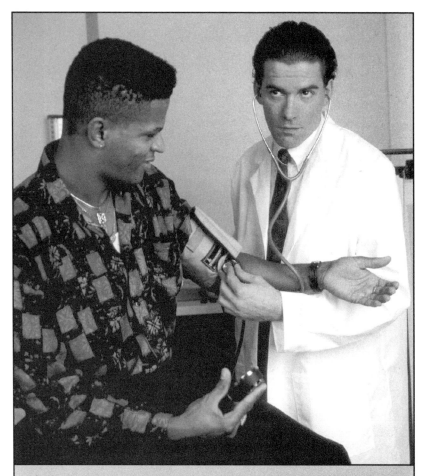

Black Americans are three times as likely as whites to develop severe high blood pressure, according to the American Heart Association.

Recent research has focused on the possible link between severe anxiety and stunted growth.

and three times as likely to suffer severe high blood pressure. "But even if a black and a white have the same degree of hypertension," Dimsdale says, "blacks have six times the severity of associated organ damage." There are several possible explanations that, alone or in combination, might account for this, including group differences in genetics, diet, and medical treatment.

Another possibility, which Dimsdale is currently exploring, is that there is a crucial difference among groups in their reactivity to stressors. He and his colleagues have concentrated on four groups of people: blacks and whites, with and without high blood pressure. "We've looked at the hormones involved in stress, and we've looked at the receptors that bind to these hormones. We've looked at the motion of the heart, and we've looked at blood pressure itself. We've examined this in response to behavioral stressors and in response to pharmacologic agents that stimulate various stress systems in the body," Dimsdale says. "And in almost every analysis we've done, we've found that black hypertensives manifest a more sensitive stress response system than the other groups."

The Long and Short of Anxiety

One of the most dramatic and heartrending consequences of severe, prolonged stress is a condition known as *psychosocial dwarfism*, in which children fail to grow normally in the face of extreme emotional depriva- tion. The process of growth makes many demands on the body's resources, and, as already noted, these demands may be put on the back burner during stressful times.

A striking example of this effect was described by a pediatrician writ- ing in *Scientific American* in 1972. A woman had given birth to twins, a girl and a boy, and all was going well until she found herself unwelcomely pregnant four months later. Within a few weeks, her husband lost his job, and not long after that, he left home. Up until that time, both babies had been growing at a normal rate, with the boy progressing slightly more rapidly. However, according to the pediatrician, the woman then began expressing her anger toward the father and, unconsciously or consciously, toward the son as well. As a result, the boy's growth rate slowed to the point where, by the age of one, his height was only that of a seven-month- old. The boy was put in the hospital, where he began to regain lost ground. In the meantime, his father returned home. After being released to this happier environment, the boy continued to improve, and by his second birthday, he had caught up in size to his sister.

More recently, researchers at the University of North Carolina in Chapel Hill and Wayne State University in Detroit have been looking at how less severe *anxiety* problems—things such as social phobias and panic disorders—may be associated with stunted growth. In preliminary results presented at the 1995 meeting of the American Psychosomatic Society, the researchers reported that people who were abnormally short during childhood due to a growth-hormone deficiency appeared to be at increased risk for developing anxiety disorders in adulthood. The researchers noted that at least part of the association could be due to the bad social experiences short people may have. However, the data suggest that something else is also occurring, perhaps involving the interaction between anxiety and *growth hormone*—that is, the pituitary hormone that largely regulates the growth process. Further research is now under way.

An Equal and Opposite Reaction

If the sympathetic nervous system were allowed to go unopposed, it would quickly wreak havoc. Fortunately, the other half of the autonomic nervous system—the parasympathetic half—is around to help the body compensate for periods of high arousal. You've probably noticed that after a big meal, you feel dull and drowsy. That's the parasympathetic nervous system in action.

Where the sympathetic nervous system diverts blood away from the digestive tract and to the muscles, the parasympathetic does the opposite. Where the sympathetic nervous system speeds up the heart rate, the parasympathetic slows it down. In addition, the parasympathetic nervous system lowers blood pressure, decreases breathing rate, increases energy storage, promotes growth, and generally induces relaxation. Stress management techniques from meditation to biofeedback to hypnosis aim to elicit this positive parasympathetic state.

Before going further, however, it's worth noting that parasympathetic activation isn't all good, any more than sympathetic arousal is all bad. Just as overactivity of the stress response can lead to disease, so can underactivity. Among the disorders that may possibly be related to an abnormally decreased stress response are inflammatory diseases, such as rheumatoid arthritis; certain types of depression, such as seasonal depression; chronic fatigue syndrome; and hypothyroidism (underactivity of the thyroid gland).

Rest and Relaxation

The set of physiological changes that offset those of the stress response are often referred to as the *relaxation response.* This term was coined by Herbert Benson, M.D., an associate professor of medicine at Harvard Medical School and president of the Mind/Body Medical Institute at New England Deaconess Hospital.

In 1968, Benson and his colleagues were studying high blood pressure in animals when they were approached by some devotees of *transcendental meditation,* a form of meditation that became popular in the United States during the 1960s. In TM, as it's called, you sit in a comfortable position while mentally repeating a special word, phrase, or sound, called a *mantra.* The meditators insisted that they could lower their blood pressure through meditation, and eventually they convinced a reluctant Benson to put their claims to the test.

Benson and his associates outfitted the meditators with devices to track a number of physiological measures, from breath rate to brain waves. The subjects then sat quietly, getting used to the equipment. In an hour or so, when the subjects were in a resting state, the researchers took measurements for 20 minutes. After that, the subjects were asked to meditate for 20 minutes, during which measurements continued to be taken. Lastly, the subjects were asked to return to their normal way of thinking, as measurements continued for a final 20 minutes. Thus, the study included premeditation, meditation, and postmeditation periods. The subjects changed only their thoughts from one period to the next, not their resting position.

Ironically, the anticipated drop in blood pressure failed to materialize, possibly because the subjects tended to have low blood pressure in the first place. However, there was a marked decrease during meditation in several aspects of metabolism. The subjects consumed 17 percent less oxygen and produced less carbon dioxide. Their respiratory rate slowed down by about three breaths per minute, and the total amount of air moving in and out of the lungs declined. In addition, there was a sharp drop in blood lactate during meditation. High levels of this chemical have been linked with anxiety and agitation, and low levels with peaceful feelings. Also, brain wave patterns changed in the meditating subjects.

There were more low-frequency alpha, theta, and delta waves, which are associated with rest and relaxation, and fewer high-frequency beta waves, which are associated with wakefulness.

Although these results were impressive, it was still uncertain how long the effects of meditation might last. Benson and his colleagues addressed this issue in a 1982 study published in *Science*. Half of the subjects elicited the relaxation response during two 20-minute sessions a day, while the other half spent the same amount of time just sitting quietly. The researchers found that, in people who regularly elicited the relaxation response, the body was less sensitive to the stress hormone norepinephrine, even during times of the day when they weren't specifically practicing the response. In other words some of the benefits of eliciting the relaxation response seemed to persist for at least several hours.

Meditations on Relaxation

According to Benson, a whole array of techniques can be used to bring about the relaxation response. At the Mind/Body Medical Institute, a variety of approaches are presented to patients, who are encouraged to pick one or more that suit them best. Whatever the chosen technique, Benson says it should be practiced for 10 to 20 minutes, once or twice a day—preferably while sitting comfortably in a quiet environment with few distractions.

"Down through history, societies have built in methods for their members to elicit the relaxation response, usually within a religious context," Benson says. "There are two basic steps necessary. The first is to repeat a word, phrase, sound, or prayer. The second is, when other thoughts come to mind, to passively disregard them and return to the repetition."

Benson says he has found examples of practices using these two steps in the literatures of Christianity, Judaism, Islam, Buddhism, Shintoism, Taoism, and Confucianism. For example, one ancient Christian prayer, which has survived to this day under the name Jesus Prayer or Prayer of the Heart, was codified in fourteenth-century Greece. The instructions were to sit in a quiet spot, repeating "Lord Jesus Christ, have mercy on me" with each exhaled breath, while disregarding other thoughts that threatened to intrude.

When You Have Got a Prayer

Such talk of prayer has traditionally been considered anathema to scientists. However, that has changed somewhat in recent years, as evidenced by the fact that one of the first grants awarded by the National Institutes of Health (NIH) Office of Alternative Medicine went to a University of New Mexico study of prayer intervention for substance abuse. A handful of conferences have lately addressed the topic also, as reported in the *Journal of the American Medical Association* in a 1995 news item titled "Should Physicians Prescribe Prayer for Health? Spiritual Aspects of Well-being Considered."

"In the past, we were told in this culture that you had to live your life in one of two ways: You could be rational and analytical, or you could be

The person repeating a prayer and disregarding other thoughts may be eliciting the relaxation response.

spiritual and religious. Now people are coming to realize that life need not be lived in this split-off, schizophrenic manner," says Larry Dossey, M.D., a former internist who writes and lectures on what might be called the mind-body-spirit link. Dossey is author of the popular 1993 book *Healing Words: The Power of Prayer and the Practice of Medicine.*

Spirituality is a person's inward sense of something greater than the individual or of meaning that transcends the immediate circumstances, while *religion* is the outward manifestation of such feelings. Dossey argues that both are fitting subjects for experimental studies.

Dossey and others distinguish between two kinds of prayer: *petitionary prayer,* in which you pray for yourself, and *intercessory prayer,* in which you pray for some distant person or thing. "Petitionary prayer fits neatly within the framework of mind-body medicine," says Dossey, who notes that this is the kind of prayer described by Benson. However, Dossey's contention, which is controversial among many practitioners of both science and religion, is that the reputed healing power of intercessory prayer can and should be examined in controlled research as well.

Whether prayer is thought of as an appeal to a higher power, a means of evoking the relaxation response, or both, doctors would probably do well to heed their patients' beliefs. For example, in a 1994 survey published in the *Journal of Family Practice,* 48 percent of the 203 hospital patients interviewed said they would like their physician to pray with them, and 42 percent said physicians should ask their patients about faith-healing experiences. Yet, although 77 percent of those surveyed said physicians should consider their patients' spiritual needs, 80 percent said their physician rarely or never discussed religious beliefs.

Bubble-Wrap Therapy

Meditation, whether practiced within a religious context or not, is a well-known stress management technique, but by no means the only one. A unique 1992 study from Western New England College in Springfield, Mass., described another method of reducing stress that many of us have already discovered for ourselves: popping the sealed-plastic air capsules in "bubble-wrap" packaging material. College students filled out checklists designed to measure their mood at the beginning of the study, after waiting for five minutes, and after popping two sheets of bubble-wrap. As predicted, the students reported feeling more energized, calmer, and less tired after popping the bubbles than after merely waiting.

How valid are more conventional approaches to managing stress? And how useful are they for treating or preventing a variety of stress-related medical conditions? The latter question has recently prompted a number of controlled, randomized clinical trials. The results are not always easy to interpret, however. For example, a major study, the Trials of Hypertension Prevention, is looking at patients with high normal blood pressure. The results of Phase I of the trials, published in 1992, compared 242 patients who received special training in stress management techniques with 320 who did not. Among the techniques taught to patients in the training group were slow breathing, progressive muscle relaxation, imagery, and stretching. After 18 months, the researchers concluded that stress management failed to reduce blood pressure significantly.

However, the picture is more complicated than it may at first appear. Among other things, critics, including Benson, have pointed out that the researchers made no attempt to determine whether stress was affecting the subjects' blood pressure in the first place. Just as weight reduction is not useful to those who aren't overweight, critics have noted, stress reduction may not be helpful to people who aren't very stressed.

The moral: Even in large studies published in respected journals—the one above appeared in the *Journal of the American Medical Association,* for instance—the results can be open to differing interpretations. In the three chapters that follow, we'll examine the results of numerous studies on the effectiveness of mind-body therapies—and we'll always try to look at them with a critical eye.

Mind on the Mend:
Meditation, Hypnosis, and Biofeedback

CLEARWATER, FLA., July 1995—A press release from the Michael A.B. Stivers' Breast Enlargement Course touts a technique for increasing bust size through hypnosis. Stivers has performed live demonstrations on more than 200 radio and TV talk shows, and he has plans for a larger demonstration in Las Vegas. He is currently marketing "breast enhancement hypnosis tapes."

n recent decades, a wide variety of serious and not-so-serious ways of exploiting the link between feeling and healing have been tried. Collectively known as *mind-body interventions,* these range from meditation and hypnosis to imagery and biofeedback, and from cognitive therapy and support groups to music therapy and humor. The past 30 years have brought an explosion of interest in these areas—and, as in so many other current booms in medicine, the impetus has been dollars as often as sense.

The fact is, mind-body medicine can be smart business. A 1995 study that makes this point was coauthored by Nicholas Cummings, Ph.D., president of the Foundation for Behavioral Health in South San Francisco, Calif. Cummings and his colleagues at the foundation randomly assigned Medicaid enrollees in Hawaii to either have eligibility for extra mental health benefits or not. Those who used the extra benefits and received mental health care reduced their annual medical costs by 9.5 to

21 percent, and these savings were stable for at least 18 months. In contrast, the annual medical costs of those who never used the extra benefits increased by 15 percent.

Health insurers, among others, are starting to take note of the savings mind-body interventions may bring. California-based

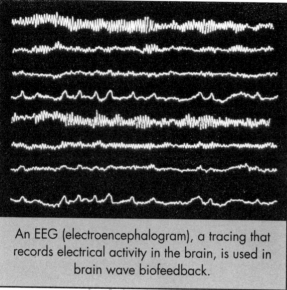

An EEG (electroencephalogram), a tracing that records electrical activity in the brain, is used in brain wave biofeedback.

↙ out of business

American Western Life Insurance Company, for instance, offers a "wellness plan" that covers such services as biofeedback, guided imagery, hypnotherapy, psychotherapy, and social work.

For the patient, therapeutic efficacy undoubtedly is even more important than cost-effectiveness. In a 1995 review of the medical literature, Fawzy Fawzy, M.D., a psychiatrist at the University of California, Los Angeles (UCLA), and his colleagues evaluated the usefulness of a variety of mind-body interventions in cancer care. The authors divided such interventions into four categories: (1) education, in which the patients are given information about their disease and its treatment; (2) training, in which the patients are taught such techniques as hypnosis, meditation, and biofeedback; (3) individual psychotherapy, in which the patients are provided counseling on a one-to-one basis; and (4) group interventions, in which the patients are given education, training, and/or psychotherapy in a group setting. The authors concluded that all of these approaches, alone or in combination, can benefit people with cancer to a statistically significant degree when used in conjunction with standard medical care.

Take Two Sugar Pills and Call Me

Controlled studies to assess how well mind-body therapies work are relatively new. However, doctors have long capitalized on the human capacity for self-healing. In Western medicine, inactive treatments whose healing power derives only from a patient's belief in their effectiveness are called placebos. The strength of the *placebo effect* is shown by the fact that the U.S. Food and Drug Administration and all major medical journals require that new drugs be tested against a *placebo*—in this situation, a dummy medication given to patients as if it were the real thing. The purpose of placebos in drug trials is to help researchers distinguish the specific benefits of a medication from the nonspecific benefits of being given *something* and believing it will work.

Patent medicines. Historically, most medicines have worked for some patients, often by the placebo effect.

At one point or another, popular remedies have included everything from eunuch fat to unicorn horn. What is most remarkable about these remedies is not that they have now been discredited, but that they ever worked for some of the people some of the time. In 1993, Alan Roberts, Ph.D., a medical psychologist at the Scripps Clinic and Research Foundation in La Jolla, Calif., reviewed a group of medical and surgical treatments that were thought to be effective when they were initially reported in the literature, but that were later shown to be ineffective. The invalidated treatments included an operation called glomectomy for bronchial asthma; a procedure involving freezing of the stomach lining for ulcers; and a drug called levamisole, a procedure using lights and dyes, and organic solvents for herpes. Roberts and his colleagues found that, in uncontrolled clinical trials when both doctors and patients believed the treatments worked, the average reported effectiveness was 40 percent excellent and 30 percent good—despite the fact that all five treatments were later proved worthless in themselves.

On an individual level, a famous case showing the importance of patient beliefs was that of "Mr. Wright," who suffered from a cancer of the lymphatic tissue called lymphosarcoma. His story was recorded for posterity in the presidential address delivered at the annual meeting of the Society for Projective Techniques in 1957. This desperately ill man begged his doctors to try a particular experimental drug. Within days, his condition improved dramatically. However, soon the newspapers reported that this "wonder drug" was not really all it had been cracked up to be. After two months of good health, Wright's condition began to deteriorate again in the face of the bad publicity. His doctor, suspecting that Wright's relapse was due to a loss of faith, reassured the patient and injected him with what he called a "new super-refined, double-strength" form of the drug. Sure enough, Wright improved remarkably again—even though this time he had been injected with nothing more than sterile water. All was well until the American Medical Association issued a statement calling the drug worthless. Soon afterward, Wright checked into a hospital and promptly died.

Meditate on It

In a broad sense, mind-body interventions can be thought of as an attempt to consciously channel the forces underlying the placebo effect. One of the best known of these approaches is *meditation,* a self-directed

A Science Writer's Tips for Science Readers

When you read about research in newspapers, magazines, or books—even this book—it's not always easy to judge the strength of the evidence upon which a statement is made or the applicability of a finding to your personal situation. Nor is it always simple to estimate the magnitude of effects, associations, risks, and costs based on the limited information given. However, understanding the following concepts can help you be a better informed consumer of science news, says Victor Cohn, former science editor at the *Washington Post* and author of the classic guidebook *News & Numbers: A Guide to Reporting Statistical Claims and Controversies in Health and Other Fields.*

- **The certainty of uncertainty.** "All science and virtually all orderly knowledge are uncertain," Cohn says. "We can only say, here's what we know today." Tomorrow we may discover something quite different.
- **The role of *probability*.** "We deal with this uncertainty by the rules of probability," says Cohn. Probability is just an estimate of what is likely to happen, based on the available evidence.
- **The *power* of large numbers.** In statistics, power refers to the probability of finding an effect if one exists. A larger sample size confers greater statistical power. In general, a sample of one makes a story, not a study.
- **The danger of *bias*.** "Bias in statistics doesn't mean prejudice," explains Cohn. It refers to factors that haven't been considered,

practice for relaxing the body and calming the mind. The degree to which this practice has penetrated mainstream American society can be seen at the Miami International Airport, which boasts its own "meditation room" to soothe the nerves of stressed-out travelers.

One 1987 study published in *Psychosomatic Medicine* compared five

In statistics, a larger sample size confers greater statistical power.

but that may present alternative explanations for the results of an experimental study.

- **The inevitability of** *variability*. "Everything that is examined varies from moment to moment and examination to examination," says Cohn. "That's one reason why no two studies ever produce exactly the same results."
- **The hierarchy of studies.** All studies are not created equal. Cohn says that keeping the above concepts in mind while reading can help you sort out the good science from the irrelevant, the insignificant, and the just plain bad.

years of medical insurance records from about 2,000 regular participants in transcendental meditation with those of about 600,000 members of the same insurance carrier. The two groups had similar benefits and deductibles. Yet the meditators had lower rates of medical use for all 18 treatment categories studied except childbirth. One drawback to this study, however, is that members of the meditation group were self-selected. It's possible that people who are drawn to meditation tend to be attracted to healthier lifestyles in general.

Meditation may not be for everyone. Certain people experience panic when they try to meditate. For some, it's closing the eyes that seems to trigger trouble. In this case, the solution is simple enough: keeping the eyes open and gazing in a relaxed way at a picture or object. For others, the problem seems to be focusing on their breathing, which is an essential element in many forms of meditation. Suddenly, a lifelong and effortless process feels unfamiliar and hard. In that situation, it may help to try eliciting the relaxation response while walking or jogging.

Another possible concern involves not the practice of meditation itself, but the controversial tactics of the transcendental meditation movement. This form of meditation, described in the last chapter, was developed by Indian leader Maharishi Mahesh Yogi, who has since established a large organization in the United States. However, reporters have disputed a number of the group's claims. One journalist writing in the *Journal of the American Medical Association* in 1991 asserted that the movement had shown in its marketing practices an apparent pattern of "misinformation, deception, and manipulation."

A Mind Full of Mindfulness

There are many different schools of meditation, each advocating a slightly different approach. A particularly popular variation is mindfulness meditation, for which a leading spokesperson in the United States is Jon Kabat-Zinn, Ph.D., an associate professor of medicine at the University of Massachusetts Medical Center.

Simply put, *mindfulness* is moment-to-moment awareness. While transcendental meditation involves focusing on a special word, phrase, or sound and disregarding other thoughts, *mindfulness meditation* does the opposite: The meditator focuses on distracting thoughts or sensations when they arise. The key is to intentionally note any thoughts or feelings as they occur, but to do so nonjudgmentally. Although grounded in ancient Buddhist practice, the mindfulness technique taught by Kabat-Zinn has been stripped of its religious trappings and adapted to a medical setting at the University of Massachusetts Stress Reduction Clinic that Kabat-Zinn founded and directs.

The ancient Chinese system of exercise known as t'ai chi is considered a form of moving meditation.

"There's really nothing magical or mystical about mindfulness meditation, in that the training involves cultivating a capacity we all have to attend to present-moment experience as it unfolds," Kabat-Zinn says. Mindfulness can be practiced on an informal basis throughout the day, by simply reminding yourself to pay attention to the present moment during daily activities. However, Kabat-Zinn also teaches more formal techniques to clinic patients to help them cope with stress, pain, and disease. One of these is the *body scan,* in which people slowly and systematically move their attention up their body, from their feet to their head, observing sensations along the way. The body scan is usually done lying down and takes about 45 minutes.

More than 6,000 patients have now gone through the program at Kabat-Zinn's stress reduction clinic, and he says about 40 mindfulness-based programs are currently operating at other clinics around the country. Unfortunately, there's still a relative dearth of hard data on the physical effects of mindfulness meditation. Kabat-Zinn says that deficiency is being addressed in ongoing clinical trials involving early-stage breast cancer and the chronic skin disease psoriasis.

Hypnotic Suggestions

Another widely used technique in mind-body medicine is *hypnosis*, a state of focused relaxation in which people can be relatively unaware of, but not completely oblivious to, their surroundings. Legitimate hypnotherapy is a far cry from the swinging pocket watches and deceptive tricks of stage hypnosis. Contrary to popular belief, for example, you aren't in an impenetrable trance when hypnotized, and you don't need an elaborate ritual to leave the state. Likewise, people can't be hypnotized involuntarily or forced to follow suggestions against their will.

In a sense, then, all hypnosis is really self-hypnosis, since it requires a willing subject. People are led into hypnosis by a process called *hypnotic*

A hypnotherapist with a young subject.

induction, which usually involves having them listen to *hypnotic sugges-tions* that help them focus their concentration and deepen their relaxation. People can also learn to enter this special mental state on their own, a process known as *self-hypnosis. Hypnotherapy* is an effort to harness the hypnotic state by using suggestions that boost some aspect of mental or physical health.

The issue of just what hypnosis is remains unsettled. Some influential theorists such as psychologist Theodore Barber, Ph.D.—first author of the 1974 classic *Hypnosis, Imagination, and Human Potentialities*—even dispute the notion that hypnosis involves a special state of consciousness at all. Barber argues that people respond to suggestions and experience the phenomena we associate with hypnosis only because they have positive attitudes, motivations, and expectations, and they allow themselves to think and imagine along suggested lines.

Studies have indicated that hypnosis may affect a broad range of physical responses, including reducing bleeding in hemophilia, lessening the severity of asthma attacks, controlling reactions to allergens such as poison ivy, and producing skin blisters and bruises. In one interesting 1994 study from the University of Vermont involving 100 pregnant women whose fetuses were in the breech position close to term, hypnotherapy was even used to change the position of their babies prior to birth.

Among the most frequently mentioned uses for hypnotherapy is pain management. In one often-cited study headed by Case Western Reserve pediatrician Karen Olness, M.D., 28 children between the ages of 6 and 12 who suffered from migraines were given either medication or a placebo for three months. Next they switched for a second three months, so that those who had previously received medication got the placebo and vice versa. Then they all were trained in self-hypnosis and asked to use it for a final three months. Self-hypnosis reduced the number of headaches recorded—from 15 per child during the medication phase, on average, to 6 during the self-hypnosis phase.

A Brief History of Hypnotism

Although hypnosis has enjoyed something of a renaissance in recent decades, its use in Western medicine dates back to the 1770s. That's when a Viennese physician in France named Franz Anton Mesmer first began experimenting with a therapy called magnetism, in which specially designed magnets were placed on the patient. It was an effort to stir up a vital fluid, termed *animal magnetism*, that Mesmer believed was present in the body. Eventually, Mesmer realized that the true healing force lay not so much in the paraphernalia as in himself, so he began concentrating on literally entrancing his patients. While the patients were in a trance, Mesmer would pass his hands over the affected body parts, often producing startling results.

Viennese physician Franz Anton Mesmer.

Within a few years, though, the medical establishment moved to discredit Mesmer, whose popularity was exceeded only by the extravagance of his claims. He was denounced as a quack and sank into obscurity. The word *mesmerism* survived, however, to describe the hypnotic technique he used to "mesmerize" patients. And we still use the phrase "animal magnetism" to describe the charismatic presence Mesmer must have displayed.

A century later, the scientific study of hypnosis was revived by French neurologist Jean Martin Charcot. Ironically, Charcot was convinced that hypnosis was a pathological condition of the nervous system found only in neurotic patients. His vivid demonstrations of hypnosis were real crowd-pleasers in nineteenth-century Paris. In one, he would summon an apparently paralyzed mental patient to the front of a lecture hall. Under hypnosis, the patient would be able to stand and walk at Charcot's bidding, but once the trance was lifted, the paralysis would return. Such patients were said to suffer from *hysteria,* in which chronic emotional problems are converted into physical symptoms.

In the twentieth century, one of the most influential proponents of medical hypnosis was the late American psychotherapist Milton Erickson, M.D. Today many, but by no means all, hypnotherapists consider themselves "Ericksonian" disciples. Among other things, Erickson used hypnotherapy to manage pain in patients with intractable diseases such as cancer.

The Hypnosis-Warts Link

Some of the most dramatic hypnotherapy claims have been made about skin conditions. Mark Twain wrote of the "charming" of warts in his Tom Sawyer stories. Dabney Ewin, M.D., a surgeon who is also a clinical professor of psychiatry at Tulane and Louisiana State University Medical Schools, wrote of "curing" warts in the *American Journal of Clinical Hypnosis*. Warts are caused by a viral infection of the cells in the top layer of skin. However, Ewin believes that the location and timing of a wart's appearance is often influenced by psychological factors.

For example, a 17-year-old boy came to see Ewin about unsightly warts on all his fingers.

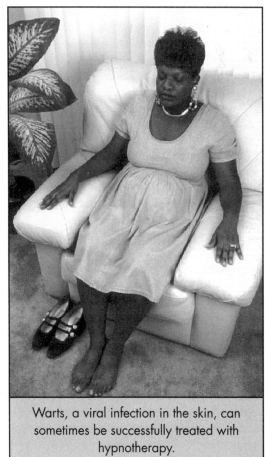

Warts, a viral infection in the skin, can sometimes be successfully treated with hypnotherapy.

Upon questioning, Ewin discovered that the warts had first appeared the previous summer, after the boy's father, a sturdy longshoreman who had been drinking, caught the boy biting his fingernails. The father grabbed him, shook him, and threatened to beat him if he ever caught him doing that again. "I thought, this will be a piece of cake," recounts Ewin, who presented this hypnotic suggestion: "Since you know that you can keep your fingers *with* warts out of your mouth, wouldn't it be all right to keep them out *without* warts?" Unfortunately, the warts didn't disappear as expected, even after several sessions. "The following summer, I got a letter from the boy, who was now at the Merchant Marine Academy," Ewin says. "Two weeks after he left home, all the warts had spontaneously gone away. The dynamics of that seem rather obvious to me: this kid wasn't taking any chances until he got away from his dad."

Researchers elsewhere have achieved success using hypnotherapy for warts. One example is a study conducted by psychologist Nicholas Spanos, Ph.D., and his colleagues at Carleton University in Ottawa, Canada. In this study of 40 adults, the subjects were randomly divided into four groups of 10, each of which received either hypnotic suggestion, applications of salicylic acid (a standard treatment), applications of a placebo, or no treatment. After six weeks, only the hypnotic subjects had lost more warts than the no-treatment controls.

The Hypnosis-Surgery Link

Another area that has garnered considerable attention is the use of hypnotic suggestion in conjunction with surgery. A fascinating paper in the annals of hypnotherapy, published in 1980 by a dentist from Waterloo, Ontario, gives a first-person account of what it's like to undergo major surgery with self-hypnosis as the sole anesthetic agent. This dentist had been using hypnosis with his patients for several years. When the time came to have his own gallbladder removed, he decided to put his knowledge to the ultimate test. He later reported that, at the time the initial incision was made, he felt a "flowing sensation." As the operation progressed, he mentally directed that sensation to any area where it was needed, while remaining totally aware of every step in the procedure. When the final stitches were in place, he triumphantly walked to his room.

On a less sensational but rather more sensible level, suggestion has been used to promote faster recovery after surgery. One prominent researcher in this area is Henry Bennett, Ph.D., a psychologist in the anesthesiology department at the University of California, Davis, Medical Center.

In a 1993 study, Bennett and his colleagues randomly assigned 40 patients who were about to undergo abdominal surgery to one of two groups: one that was simply given general information and instructions on how to clear their lungs after surgery, and another that was given general information along with specific suggestions that their gastrointestinal system would soon resume functioning following the operation. Among the suggestions given to the latter group was: "Your stomach will churn and growl, your intestines will pump and gurgle, and you will be hungry soon after your surgery."

"The intestines don't much like to be touched during surgery," Bennett says. The usual result is ileus, in which the bowel stops contracting. Ileus is one thing that prolongs postoperative hospital stays, since a patient can't return to normal eating until the bowel is moving again. In Bennett's study, this happened after just 2.6 days in patients who had been given specific presurgical suggestions, compared to 4.2 days in patients from the other group. In addition, patients in the suggestion group left the hospital an average of 1.5 days sooner than the others, which resulted in a savings of about $1,200 per patient.

Biofeedback Feedback

Yet another common mind-body intervention is *biofeedback,* a treatment method that uses monitoring instruments to feed back to patients accurate and immediate physiological information, usually in auditory or visual form. The goal is to enable patients to gain some voluntary control over physiological processes of which they are normally unaware. By listening to or looking at the monitoring device, a patient can often learn by trial and error to control such processes as blood pressure, body temperature, brain wave activity, and gastrointestinal function.

In the last few years, major advances in instrumentation have raised biofeedback's stock among scientists. Thanks to modern computers and high-tech electronics, some equipment can now continuously store data and easily allow patients to compare their results against both popula-

A biofeedback session.

tion norms and their personal results from previous sessions. This new-and-improved equipment can also make finer distinctions, clueing patients in to even minuscule changes in body function. Biofeedback has come a long way from its rather modest roots in the 1960s, when experimental psychologists such as Neal Miller, Ph.D., of Rockefeller University in New York City, first began wiring people up in studies of physiological self-control.

Biofeedback is an outgrowth of *psychophysiology*, the study of the mind's effects on physiological processes. According to the Association for Applied Psychophysiology and Biofeedback, some of the conditions for which "appropriate research" has found that biofeedback is an "established, non-experimental treatment" are asthma, epilepsy, hyperactivity, high blood pressure, migraine, tension headache, incontinence, irritable bowel syndrome, motion sickness, whiplash, and lower back strain.

At the beginning of a biofeedback session, the therapist usually takes baseline recordings, to see how the patient's body responds under standardized conditions without biofeedback. Having these data for later comparison helps the therapist evaluate how well treatment is working. The biofeedback portion of the session typically lasts 30 to 60 minutes. The number of sessions required depends upon such factors as the type, number, and duration of the symptoms being treated; the amount and type of any medication being used; and the age, motivation, and learning ability of the patient. However, it usually takes six to 20 office sessions to meet relaxation goals, while other goals such as the treatment of chronic pain may take dozens of sessions.

Picking Up the Body's Signals

Frequently used types of biofeedback include:

- **Skin temperature feedback.** This indicates blood flow changes from the dilation and constriction of blood vessels—the more constricted the blood vessels, the less blood flows through them, and so the cooler the skin. A temperature sensor, called a *thermistor,* is taped to the skin, usually on a finger. This is mainly used for conditions involving the cardiovascular system, such as high blood pressure, migraine, and Raynaud's disease, a disorder in which the blood vessels supplying the extremities are extra-sensitive to cold.
- *Electromyographic feedback. Electromyography* detects electrical activity related to spasms or tension in particular muscles. Sensors can be placed over any appropriate muscle group. This allows a person to observe minute changes in muscle tension, helping them to relax or self-regulate the muscles involved. Among its uses are for tension headaches, teeth grinding, and torticollis, a condition in which the neck turns or jerks involuntarily to one side due to unwanted sustained muscle contractions.
- *Electrodermal response.* The electrical conductivity of the skin is known as the electrodermal response. As sympathetic nervous system arousal rises, so does sweat gland activity for many people. Conductance of electricity increases with greater sweating, because electrical current flows more easily through the salty moisture on the skin's surface. Sensors are attached to the palm side of the fin-

gers or hand. Among it uses is for hyperhidrosis, a condition characterized by overactive sweat glands.

- **Breathing feedback.** This assesses breath rate, volume, rhythm, and location in the chest and abdomen. Some therapists place sensors around the chest and abdomen. Others measure air flow from the mouth and nose. The goal is to help a person learn to take slower, deeper, lower, and more regular breaths using the abdominal muscles. This is often used for treating asthma.

- **Brain wave feedback.** *Electroencephalography* uses a brain wave tracing known as an electroenephalogram (EEG) to record electrical activity in the brain. Sensors are positioned on the scalp. Among the applications for this form of biofeedback that are currently being developed are epilepsy, hyperactivity, alcoholism, other addictive disorders, insomnia, and brain injury.

The Biofeedback-Diabetes Link

Biofeedback often plays a role in relaxation treatments whose aim is to lower the physical tension and arousal that accompany many stress-related conditions. One promising use for biofeedback-aided relaxation training is helping diabetics control their glucose, or blood sugar. A key figure in this field is Angele McGrady, Ph.D., a professor of psychiatry at the Medical College of Ohio.

"My work on diabetes actually started by accident," McGrady says. A 36-year-old woman was referred to McGrady for the treatment of anxiety. This woman happened to have type I diabetes, the insulin-dependent form of the disease that results from the body's failure to produce *insulin*, the hormone that allows glucose to enter body cells and fuel them. When glucose cannot enter the cells, it builds up in the blood and the cells starve to death. That's why people with type I diabetes must take daily insulin injections and keep close tabs on their blood glucose levels. McGrady's patient had a particularly erratic case of diabetes that typically put her in the hospital several times a year. However, as her biofeedback-aided relaxation training with McGrady went along, the woman noticed that her condition began to stabilize. When McGrady checked, she discovered that the woman's blood glucose did indeed decrease as biofeedback progressed, in terms of both weekly averages and the size of the fluctuations.

The experience prompted McGrady to conduct a pair of controlled studies on the use of biofeedback to manage insulin-dependent diabetes. In one, 18 adults with type I diabetes were randomly assigned to biofeedback or control groups. After 10 sessions of biofeedback-aided relaxation training, the researchers found that the treated subjects had lower average blood glucose levels than the controls. However, because the treatment included general relaxation training

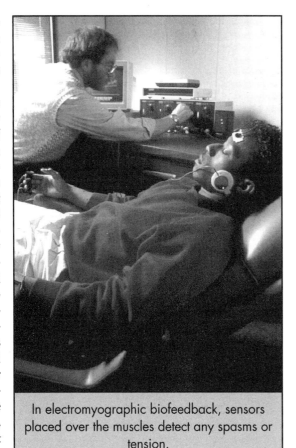

In electromyographic biofeedback, sensors placed over the muscles detect any spasms or tension.

and stress management counseling in addition to electromyographic and skin temperature biofeedback, it's not clear which components actually brought about the change.

Stress does seem to make diabetes tougher to control. For people with type II diabetes—the kind in which the body still produces insulin, but simply fails to make enough or to use it properly—one obvious factor is the drop in insulin production that occurs as part of the stress response. For people with type I diabetes, who don't make insulin in the first place, this isn't an issue. However, stress may still affect their levels of blood glucose via the nervous and endocrine systems. In addition, people with diabetes may be more likely to forget to take their medication or otherwise take care of themselves during times of stress.

Just Relax!

The three mind-body interventions described so far—meditation, hypnosis, and biofeedback—share something in common: All can be used to induce a state of relaxation. Two other techniques that are sometimes used to elicit the relaxation response are autogenic training and progressive muscle relaxation. *Autogenic training,* originated by German physician Johannes Schultz, M.D., combines exercises centered on feelings of heaviness and warmth in the limbs with a passive focus on breathing. *Progressive muscle relaxation,* developed by American physiologist Edmund Jacobson, M.D., includes exercises involving the alternate tensing and relaxing of muscle groups.

As Jacobson originally described progressive muscle relaxation, it could take more than 40 individual sessions to learn the technique. Later practitioners have streamlined his approach so that fewer sessions are needed. A 1993 paper from the University of Kentucky looked at the results of such abbreviated training reported for 29 experiments published since 1980. These results were subjected to *meta-analysis,* a statistical procedure for combining the results of several compatible studies to draw conclusions. The researchers found that progressive muscle relaxation training seemed to be an effective treatment for a variety of disorders ranging from tension headache to the side effects of chemotherapy. In general, the best results were achieved when patients were trained individually, rather than in a group, and were provided with audiotapes for home practice.

While such techniques emphasize how the mind is operating, others concentrate more on what the mind is thinking. In the next chapter, we'll take a look at imagery and the various forms of psychotherapy, mind-body approaches that are especially concerned with the contents of a person's thoughts.

More Mind Menders:
Imagery and Psychotherapy

CHIMAYO, N.M., April 1995—About 60,000 pilgrims were expected to visit this northern New Mexico village of 2,000 people for Holy Week, according to the Associated Press. Some spent days walking from Albuquerque, 90 miles away, while others trekked 30 miles through the night from Santa Fe. They came to a simple adobe church, where they waited their turn to kneel by a hole in the floor and scoop up a handful of dirt reputed to have remarkable healing powers.

here is something in the human spirit that wants to believe in miracles. It is this belief that draws more than 4 million people a year to the famous shrine at Lourdes in the French Pyrenees. In 1858, a 14-year-old girl reputedly saw a vision of a woman in white there who instructed her to dig in a sandy spot, where the girl discovered a spring. Word soon spread that the white-clad woman had been the Blessed Virgin Mary, and people began flocking to the spring whose waters were said to miraculously cure the sick. In the intervening years, it is estimated that more than 2 million diseased and injured people have been among the pilgrims who traveled to the site.

In fact, tales of miraculous cures are so common within the Catholic Church that a special set of criteria for evaluating such claims has been in place since 1735. In the case of Lourdes, an international medical committee rules whether "medically and scientifically inexplicable" cures have indeed occurred, while the church decides which such cures should be deemed "miraculous." Cases that have passed both of these hurdles include those of more than 60 people who were previously afflicted with such serious conditions as tuberculosis, multiple sclerosis, and cancer.

It's interesting to note how the number and type of cures at Lourdes have changed over the decades along with medical science. Although there were 7 certified miraculous cures in the 1940s and 10 in the 1950s, there was only 1 in each of the next two decades. Thanks to medical progress, some conditions, such as tuberculosis, that previously met the criterion of being "incurable or unlikely to respond to treatment" no longer qualify. Our standard for miracles has risen.

Miracle Cures and Remarkable Recoveries

Many scientists prefer to talk about *spontaneous remissions* rather than miracles. This refers to a patient's unexpected improvement that occurs in the absence of a known cause; in other words, without any medical treatment or after only partial or palliative treatment that should not have produced the change. According to the Institute of Noetic Sciences, a controversial organization devoted to the study of consciousness, the mind and "human potential," over 3,500 accounts of spontaneous remission have appeared in 830 medical journals from around the world since 1846. (While the institute has supported what is probably the most extensive study of spontaneous remission to date, it's worth noting that this organization also delves into such unscientific subjects as extrasensory perception and psychic "channeling.")

In fact, while the spontaneous remission of a serious disease such as cancer may be unlikely in any specific patient, it is not uncommon in patients as a group. A small percentage of cancer patients, for instance, will generally get better no matter what, for reasons that are unexplainable based on current medical knowledge. That doesn't mean there isn't a reason—just that it isn't yet recognized and understood. As Saint Augustine put it 16 centuries ago: "Miracles do not happen in contradiction of nature, but in contradiction of what we know about nature."

In evaluating therapies, it's important to keep in mind that some purported cures following any treatment regimen are likely to be due to coincidence rather than to cause and effect. In other situations, the patient may have been misdiagnosed in the first place. And in yet other cases, the disease may still be progressing silently unknown to the patient. Cancer, for example, can go through phases during which the symptoms improve or even disappear. If the disease isn't properly treated, however, it can continue to advance during this time and reemerge later at a deadlier stage.

The Mind's Eye and Ear

One mind-body intervention that has been much publicized—and highly controversial—in cancer patients is *imagery*. This refers to the imagining of something experienced through one of the senses: sight, hearing, smell, taste, touch, or movement. Although the term is often used synonymously with *visualization*, this is misleading, because the latter really refers only to something that is seen through the mind's eye, while imagery encompasses all of the senses.

Although imagery is frequently used in conjunction with hypnosis, the two are actually distinct techniques. Briefly stated, hypnosis is a state of mind, while imagery is a mental activity. It's certainly possible to have one without the other. However, when hypnotic suggestions are given, they often take the form of imagery. Another form of therapy that has a strong imagery component is autogenic training, in which you imagine that your limbs feel warm and heavy.

Imagery is taught both individually and in groups, often with a particular aim in mind, such as bolstering the immune system. There are three major ways in which imagery can be employed in a medical setting:

- *Diagnostic imagery.* This refers to imagery that is elicited as part of the health evaluation process. The patient is asked to describe his or her physical condition in sensory terms. The therapist can then use this information for custom-designing both mental rehearsal and therapeutic intervention strategies.
- *Mental rehearsal.* This refers to imagery that is practiced before medical procedures to relieve anxiety, pain, and side effects. Surgery, for instance, can be mentally rehearsed before the event so that the patient is prepared and unhindered by frightening fantasies. Such imagery is often part of natural childbirth training.
- *Therapeutic imagery.* This refers to imagery that is aimed at exerting a direct or indirect impact on health. Such images are intended to either enhance the healing process or distract and relax the patient. Among other things, imagery has been used for relieving

the nausea associated with chemotherapy, promoting weight gain in cancer patients, and controlling pain in various situations.

Jeanne Achterberg, Ph.D., a psychology professor at the Saybrook Institute in San Francisco, has helped popularize imagery with her books in which it is seen as a possible basis for modern healing rituals. Achterberg argues that all societies develop rituals to help their members cope with life's passages. Contemporary Western society is no exception. However, she contends that the medicalized rituals that now go along with such milestones as birth, pregnancy, menopause, and death may not be very soul-satisfying. Imagery, she suggests, can be the source of self-generated healing rituals that better fulfill this deeply human need.

The Imagery-Cancer Link

One of the best-known and most-debated books in mind-body medicine is *Getting Well Again,* a 1978 best seller that describes the use of

qualified people. Articles in leading journals undergo peer
review prior to publication.
- **Provider's credentials.** What training and experience does the
  health care provider have in this area? At a bare minimum,
  check that the person is certified or licensed to practice in the
  field.
- **Treatment costs.** What is the total cost of the treatment, and
  how will it be billed? Will insurance cover it? Remember that
  many alternative treatments are not reimbursable by health
  insurance.

A final reminder: Discuss all treatments with your physician,
who may have additional insights into the approach to share with
you. At the very least, your physician needs to know about any alternative therapies you may be trying in order to have a complete picture of your treatment plan.

imagery and other psychological approaches in cancer treatment. Lead
author Carl Simonton, M.D., a radiation oncologist, and his coauthors
note that imagery involves a highly personal symbolic language that
varies from individual to individual.

However, the authors also outline in the book several qualities that
they claim are common to effective cancer-fighting images: The cancer
cells should be pictured as weak and confused, they maintain, while the
treatment should be seen as strong and powerful. The healthy cells
should be visualized as having no trouble repairing any damage the
treatment might do. In addition, a vast army of white blood cells should
be imagined as overwhelming the cancer cells. These white blood cells
should be pictured as eager for battle and quick to find and destroy cancer cells. The cancer cells should then be seen as flushing naturally from
the body. By the end of imagery, the authors write, patients should visu-
alize themselves as healthy and free of cancer, ready to reach their goals
and fulfill their purpose in life.

Today Simonton is founder and medical director of the Simonton

Cancer Center in Pacific Palisades, Calif. His work still attracts patients and clinicians from around the world. However, in the two decades since Simonton began his imagery work, no definitive study has ever been done to show whether this brand of imagery exercise really does promote tumor regression.

Of course, there are other reasons why imagery might benefit cancer patients. For example, it might help a patient cope with anxiety, pain, and the unpleasant side effects of chemotherapy and radiation therapy. Simonton believes it's realistic to expect "that we can improve the quality of our lives, that we can significantly impact the quality of our death, and that we can significantly impact the course of our disease." What's unrealistic, he

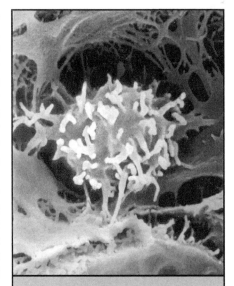

The human immune system has several defenses against cancer, including killer T cells, natural killer cells, and macrophages. In this micrograph, a macrophage is seen in the liver.

says, is to enter into treatment with the "inappropriate expectation" that you're definitely going to be well in a set time.

One charge leveled by critics is that people who don't get better might become depressed, because they feel they weren't mentally strong enough to defeat their own cancer. Among those who have voiced concerns is Jimmie Holland, M.D., chief of the psychiatry service at Memorial Sloan-Kettering Cancer Center in New York City and a founder of the field of *psychooncology*—the study of psychological aspects of cancer. Simonton acknowledges that such feelings were indeed a problem with some of his early patients, but he says that he is now "addressing how to effectively deal with guilt as part of the routine process of counseling."

The Relaxation Techniques-Infertility Link

Imagery should complement, not replace, traditional medical treatment. In addition, imagery is usually combined with other mind-body interventions. One promising combination approach that incorporates imagery is the Mind/Body Infertility Program at New England Deaconess Hospital in Boston. The founder and director of this program is Alice Domar, Ph.D., an assistant professor of medicine at Harvard Medical School.

In 10 weekly sessions, Domar presents a variety of relaxation techniques, including visual imagery of nature scenes, meditation, autogenic training, and progressive muscle relaxation. The program also includes other elements, such as group sharing and a session on self-empathy. "We know that high levels of emotional stress can negatively affect both the female and the male reproductive systems," Domar says. "A lot of infertility patients are relatively okay psychologically until they start treatment. But the high-tech treatment itself can be acutely stressful."

Consider the couple trying in vitro fertilization. "You've got couples who scrimp and save until they finally have enough money for one cycle. So they plunk down $10,000 and go through a very tough four weeks," says Domar. "During a cycle, the average patient has at least two injections a day. Patients have to

The use of relaxation techniques may facilitate the healing process.

go in for daily blood tests and ultrasound, which may mean they're late for work. There's always a chance that a cycle will be canceled. And even if they make it through the whole cycle, there's an 80 percent chance of it not working."

"One has to wonder," says Domar, "if people were not so stressed out by the treatment, would the pregnancy rates be higher than they are now?" The answer to that question will have to await the completion of a controlled, randomized clinical trial that Domar recently began. In the meantime, she insists that she considers pregnancy in women who complete the program to be just a "nice side effect." The more immediate goal, she says, is to help infertile couples "stop living in 28-day cycles."

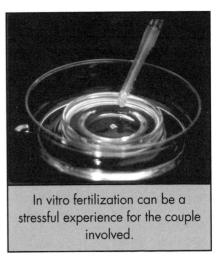

In vitro fertilization can be a stressful experience for the couple involved.

Mending the Mind

Another broad group of mind-body approaches falls under the heading of *psychotherapy*, the treatment of emotional and psychological difficulties. Among the health care practitioners who provide psychotherapy are psychiatrists, psychologists, clinical social workers, marriage and family therapists, and mental health counselors. *Behavioral medicine* is one name given to that field comprised of professionals who use psychotherapeutic techniques to alleviate medical problems. More specifically, it is the multidisciplinary field that investigates the interactions of behavior, physiological and biochemical states, and disease and mortality.

Psychotherapy can be undertaken either individually or in a group. There are literally dozens of types of therapy now practiced. Some of the major categories include:

- *Psychodynamic therapy.* This is derived from psychoanalysis and is usually directed at changing fundamental personality patterns. It seeks the root of present emotional conflicts in early childhood experiences in order to provide insight and resolution.

- *Behavior therapy.* This is aimed at changing a particular unwanted behavior. It seeks to remove whatever has been reinforcing the behavior or replace the behavior with a more desirable response. Specific instructions must be followed between sessions.
- *Cognitive therapy.* This is aimed at changing a particular unwanted behavior indirectly, by focusing on the habitual thoughts that affect how a person behaves. Cognitive therapy is closely related to and frequently combined with behavior therapy.
- *Systems therapy.* This is focused on destructive patterns in personal relationships. It may involve couples or the whole family in sessions, and it often entails assignments at home.
- *Supportive therapy.* This is directed at people who are in the grips of a major emotional crisis. It may include drug therapy as a way to help people cope with their daily demands.

Holland has identified several factors that have contributed to the new emphasis on treating the psychological side of cancer. Many apply to other

A psychotherapist and client.

diseases as well. First, she notes that society's attitude toward cancer has become less pessimistic. Second, the earlier advances in diagnosis and treatment have indeed led to more effective combinations of surgery, chemotherapy, and radiation for certain cancers. Third, there is an increased focus today on more patient-centered health care. Fourth, there is also a heightened awareness of the way psychology and behavior influence cancer risk, detection, and prevention. Fifth, psychiatry has recently begun to develop services geared specifically toward the needs of the medically ill.

Mind Over Medical Matters

Research has shown that psychotherapy can speed up the recovery process after an illness. A 1991 study headed by psychiatrist James Strain, M.D., of Mount Sinai Medical Center in New York City, looked at 452 consecutive patients aged 65 or older who were admitted to two hospitals for surgical repair of a fractured hip. It focused on the difference between *consultation psychiatry*, in which a psychiatrist is called in by the primary-care doctor only when a hospitalized patient has been identified as having an emotional problem, and *liaison psychiatry*, in which a psychiatrist is part of each patient's medical team from the start of the hospital stay. The researchers compared people admitted one year, during which only psychiatric consultation was offered, with those admitted during the next year, during which liaison therapy was offered in some units to all patients who needed it.

In liaison therapy units, psychiatrists treated the patients for any emotional or psychological problems that had arisen from their medical condition and that might interfere with their recovery. During the liaison therapy year, the average length of hospital stay was cut from 20.7 to 18.5 days at Mount Sinai and from 15.5 to 13.8 days at another hospital in Chicago.

Psychotherapy may also be able to prolong the lives of some cancer patients. One of the most influential studies ever published in mind-body medicine is a 1989 report authored by Stanford psychiatrist David Spiegel, M.D., and colleagues and published in the leading British medical journal, *The Lancet*. In the study, 86 women with advanced breast cancer were randomly assigned to either treatment or control groups. All received standard medical care, but those in the treatment group also got weekly supportive group therapy along with self-hypnosis training for pain control.

The group therapy patients were encouraged to express their feelings about the disease and its effect on their lives. The group leaders—a psychiatrist or social worker plus a therapist who had breast cancer in remission—helped to keep the members directed toward facing and grieving their losses. Physical problems were also discussed, and a self-hypnosis strategy for managing pain was taught. In addition, the members forged close bonds and urged each other to take a more active role in their own care. Ten years later, the researchers tracked down what had become of these women. They found that those in the treatment group had lived longer than did the controls, by an average of 18 months. That may not sound like much added survival time, but it was longer than any known medication or medical treatment could have been expected to provide for women whose breast cancer was so far advanced.

It's ironic that Spiegel's original goal was to disprove the idea that psychological factors can affect cancer's outcome. However, Spiegel has written that he remains leery of "the often overstated claims made by those who teach cancer patients that the right mental attitude will help to conquer the disease." Such claims can even be dangerous if they lead patients to give up accepted medical care.

The Psychotherapy-Cancer Link

Since the publication of Spiegel's findings, other researchers have also reported impressive results with cancer patients. Prominent among them is Fawzy Fawzy, M.D., a psychiatry professor at the University of California in Los Angeles.

In a 1993 paper, Fawzy and his colleagues described the long-term effects of group therapy for patients with malignant melanoma. Back in the mid-1980s, 80 patients with early-stage melanoma had been randomly assigned to either treatment or control groups. Both groups received standard medical care, took tests to assess their emotional state and coping methods, and gave blood so the researchers could check various measures of immune function. In addition, 38 treatment subjects participated in six weekly group therapy sessions.

The sessions themselves had four components: (1) education, including information on melanoma and general health; (2) stress management, including relaxation techniques; (3) coping skills, including problem-solving techniques; and (4) psychological support, from both the staff and other group members, including talks on engendering hope and discussions of family and illness-related problems.

Six months later, 35 of the treatment patients and 26 of the controls showed up for tests of their immune status. The researchers found that natural killer cell activity was increased in the treatment group. In addition, patients in this group showed less depression, fatigue, and confusion and more vigor on a test of their emotional state, as well as more active coping methods on a test of coping skills.

For the six-year follow-up study, Fawzy and his associates were able to track down 34 patients from each of the original groups. They found that 10 of those from the control group had died, versus only 3 from the treatment group—a statistically significant difference. A trend in the same direction was noted for recurrences of the disease. While these results are certainly provocative, the small number of subjects limits the degree to which they can be generalized to other patients.

One thing that is notable about this approach is the attendance rate. At the melanoma therapy sessions, attendance was almost 100 percent, and no one missed more than a single meeting. "We were really able to engage the participants, and we made sure that each session had a specific agenda that dealt with a particular topic. We gave them information that built on previous attendance," says Fawzy. More recently, Fawzy has run similar groups for people with breast cancer and AIDS. "I'm now in the process of modifying the intervention for prostate cancer patients," he says.

The Psychotherapy-Herpes Virus Link

How might psychological therapy affect physical health? There are many possible mechanisms: by decreasing stress, by reducing social isolation, by providing patient education, or by promoting healthful behaviors. However, another possibility is that, by disclosing upsetting emotions, people may be able to influence the immune system directly. Psychologist James Pennebaker, Ph.D., of Southern Methodist University in Dallas, has pioneered the study of the healing power of confiding in others. His basic conclusion is that, over time, holding back thoughts and feelings puts people at higher risk of various diseases. Confession, on the other hand, appears to be good for the body as well as the soul.

Some intriguing new research in this area comes from Brian Esterling, Ph.D., an assistant professor of medical psychology at Duke University in Durham, N.C. A 1994 study by Esterling and his colleagues included 57 college students who tested positive for Epstein-Barr virus (EBV). This is one of the herpes viruses, which, unlike other common viruses, remain in the body for life and can flare up unpredictably. EBV is thought to cause mononu-

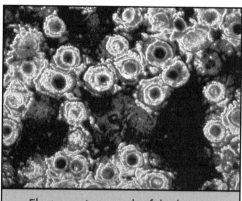

Electron micrograph of the herpes simplex virus.

cleosis. Other herpes viruses cause genital herpes, cold sores, cytomegalovirus infection, chicken pox, and shingles.

The students were randomly assigned to one of three groups. In two groups, the subjects were asked to think about a stressful event that had happened to them and that they had not disclosed to many people. They were urged to pick an event that seemed highly stressful or traumatic or about which they felt very guilty. Then some were asked to write an essay about the event at three weekly sessions, while others were asked to speak into a tape recorder about it. In the third group, the subjects spent the three sessions writing about trivial topics, such as the contents of their closets.

All the students gave blood samples about a week before the first session and a week after the last one. The researchers found that either speaking or writing about something stressful decreased EBV antibody titers, indicating better immune control over the latent virus, during the four-week study period. Subjects who *spoke* about stressful events had lower values than those who *wrote* about stressful events—who, in turn, had lower values than those who merely wrote about trivial topics.

"The students in the stressful groups talked and wrote about very personal and upsetting experiences—things such as being raped or experiencing their parents' divorce," says Esterling. "If you're put in a stressful situation like that, experiencing the negative emotions involved may be bad for you. But if you're given the chance to comfortably talk about what happened, either verbally or in written form, that seems to help your immune system somehow, at least with respect to reactivation of EBV."

Getting Your Thoughts Together

One type of psychotherapy that has provoked much interest as a mind-body treatment is cognitive therapy, developed by psychiatrist Aaron Beck, M.D., of the University of Pennsylvania. In this form of therapy, patients try to identify and correct the faulty thinking patterns that underlie their problems. Beck believes that habitual negative thoughts often limit a person's perspective on life and interfere with constructive problem-solving, thus contributing to depression and other ailments.

Such thoughts may display the traits of a pessimistic explanatory style, as defined by another notable University of Pennsylvania researcher, psychologist Martin Seligman, Ph.D. Therefore, cognitive therapy is sometimes used to help people adopt a more optimistic frame of mind. Cognitive therapy is also incorporated into many stress management programs. The assumption is that, before you can experience something as stressful, you must first process it and assign it a personal meaning. By making minor adjustments in your habitual thinking style, you may be less likely to overreact emotionally.

At the University of Miami, a cognitive-behavioral stress management program was established to help gay men cope with one of the most distressing diagnoses in modern medicine: the news that they had tested positive for the human immunodeficiency virus (HIV). The treatment program, run by psychologist Michael Antoni, Ph.D., and his colleagues, combined cognitive therapy with assertiveness training, education, and support. In a 1991 study, 47 gay men who had not yet been tested for HIV were recruited and randomly assigned to either treated or untreated control groups. Midway into the 10-week treatment program, both groups were tested for HIV, and about one-third of the men in each group tested positive. A week after learning the results in private interviews, the men returned for another blood test, this one intended to measure the impact of the news on their immune function.

The researchers found that HIV-infected men who participated in the program had increases in the levels of helper T cells and natural killer cells, while those who did not go through the program had decreases in both immune measures. In addition, of the men in the treatment group, those who attended more sessions were healthier two years later than those who came less often.

Head and Heart

The results of Antoni, Fawzy, and Spiegel all illustrate just how effective programs that combine multiple approaches can be. Another example is the ongoing program to reverse coronary heart disease established by cardiologist Dean Ornish, M.D., of the University of California in San Francisco. Ornish's work combines stress management strategies such as stretching exercises, breathing techniques, meditation, progressive muscle relaxation, and imagery with a low-fat vegetarian diet, moderate exercise, and no smoking. The results have been convincing enough that Mutual of Omaha Insurance Company now sends patients to Ornish's lifestyle centers on the theory that the enrollment fee of $5,000 a patient is a lot less than the cost of bypass surgery.

Unfortunately, such programs also show the difficulty in separating out exactly which aspects of a multifaceted approach are responsible for its effects. That may not be a fatal flaw in the eyes of patients, though, who are usually more concerned with knowing what a treatment can do than with understanding how it does it.

Yet another widely praised effort is the Commonweal Cancer Help Program in Bolinas, Calif. Cofounder and director Michael Lerner, Ph.D., is a political scientist who has been active in health issues for two decades. Among other honors, he received a prestigious MacArthur Prize Fellowship for his health-related work in 1983. Commonweal hosts six week-long retreats each year, at which participants can educate themselves to make informed choices about conventional and alternative cancer therapies. They can also partake of progressive

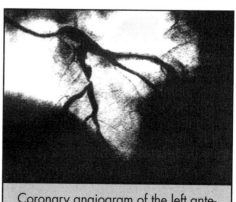

Coronary angiogram of the left anterior descending artery.

muscle relaxation, meditation, imagery, art therapy, massage, yoga, and a vegetarian diet. Each participant is encouraged to find his or her personal path to "healing," which doesn't necessarily imply a cure, but may mean a better quality of life. Because only eight people can go on each retreat, Commonweal is also committed to helping other centers start versions of their program.

Of course, just because a program is popular doesn't automatically mean it can be shown to be effective in objective testing. A case in point is the Exceptional Cancer Patients organization founded by Bernie Siegel, M.D., a surgeon in New Haven, Conn. Siegel is author of the best-selling 1986 book *Love, Medicine & Miracles: Lessons Learned About Self-Healing from a Surgeon's Experience with Exceptional Patients*. In it, he describes an approach based on small support groups of cancer patients plus invited family and friends who meet weekly for 90-minute sessions of individual and group counseling and training in relaxation, imagery, and meditation. One controversial aspect of this program is its heavy emphasis on "the will to live." In a 1993 study by Siegel and his colleagues that compared 34 ECaP participants, all women with breast cancer, to 102 nonparticipants whose disease was at a similar stage, there was no evidence of increased survival among the ECaP members.

Make Mine a Combo, Please

One noteworthy aspect of some of these combination programs is their successful mixture of psychotherapeutic and meditative techniques. This may not seem like a very revolutionary idea. However, for many decades, it was believed that psychotherapy, which was supposed to be rational and scientific, simply didn't mix with meditation, which was supposed to be irrational and spiritual.

That's a less common preconception today, thanks to influential writers such as Herbert Benson, M.D., discoverer of the relaxation response, and Joan Borysenko, Ph.D., cofounder and former director of the Mind/Body Clinic at New England Deaconess Hospital. In a 1985 paper published in the *American Journal of Psychiatry*, these authors and a colleague argue that the two forms of self-observation—psychotherapy and meditation—actually complement each other. They note that both call for systematic introspection as a means of achieving self-knowledge.

Interestingly, as medicine is moving to embrace the mind, psychotherapy is also starting to include the body. Several studies have shown that physical *exercise*—whether running, walking, or some other sport—can often ease anxiety and lift depression. There are many possible reasons why this might occur, including an improved self-image and a greater sense of personal mastery, as well as the temporary distraction from more disturbing concerns. However, there may also be biochemical explanations. It's known, for instance, that exercise affects the level of various brain chemicals, and an intense workout can trigger the release of endorphins.

Cornell psychiatrist Michael Sacks, M.D., an expert on the mental health benefits of exercise, has noted that the effect seems to be fairly short-lived, lasting from several hours to a day. Therefore, if you want to get the greatest psychological boost, Sacks suggests that a daily workout of at least 30 minutes duration may be needed—more than the three to five sessions per week of at least 20 minutes duration that are generally recommended for attaining cardiovascular fitness goals.

Running and other forms of physical exercise are an integral part of some psychological treatment programs.

Today running, yoga, dance, and other forms of exercise are an integral part of some psychological treatment regimens. And a branch of psychotherapy known as *body-oriented therapy* uses breathing techniques, movement, and manual pressure to help people release emotions that are thought to be expressed as bodily tension and restriction. Heart and soul, body and mind are slowly coming back together.

The Joy of . . . Joy:
Friends, Pets, Music, Art, and Humor

A merry heart doeth good like a medicine.
Proverbs 17:22

I made the joyous discovery that ten minutes of genuine belly laughter had an anesthetic effect and would give me at least two hours of pain-free sleep.
Norman Cousins, *Anatomy of an Illness as Perceived by the Patient: Reflections on Healing and Regeneration*, 1979

ou don't have to have a string of fancy initials after your name to make astute observations about the relationship between joy and healing. In fact, having a modern medical education has often seemed to be somewhat of a liability in this regard. In recent years, however, doctors have begun to study and establish what patients have always suspected: that laughter and joy really are the best medicine of all.

In their 1989 book *Healthy Pleasures*, psychologist Robert Ornstein, Ph.D., and physician David Sobel, M.D., put forth their own version of the Pleasure Principle: "In short, the healthiest people seem to be pleasure-loving, pleasure-seeking, pleasure-creating individuals." The authors note that the brain is generously supplied with chemicals that transmit pleasure signals from one nerve cell to another. They suggest that the human capacity for enjoyment evolved as a way to enhance survival, since healthy behaviors such as eating, reproducing, and caring for others also tend to be pleasurable.

Laughter and pleasure are among the best medicines of all.

Doing Unto Others

The 1994 book *Sound Mind, Sound Body: A New Model for Lifelong Health,* by Kenneth Pelletier, M.D., lays out a variation on this theme: "Health . . . is an inner quality that gives rise to particular health practices but cannot in itself be reduced to those practices." Pelletier, a clinical associate professor of medicine at the Stanford Center for Research in Disease Prevention, based his book on a series of extensive interviews with 53 prominent individuals whom he considered models of optimal health. He found that material wealth and a diet and exercise regimen were not sufficient to make people happy and healthy. Instead, he identified the key factor as "moving beyond purely materialistic and competitive concerns to the discovery of a deeper meaning." For Pelletier, the joy of life is in the giving. He found that all the participants in his study cited a sense of *altruism*—that is, an unselfish regard for the welfare of others—as a prime motivating force behind their active lifestyles.

In fact, such altruistic behavior may do as much for the giver as the receiver. In a classic study led by University of Michigan social psychologist James House, Ph.D., 2,754 adults from Tecumseh, Mich., were followed for 9 to 12 years. The researchers found that men who took part in volunteer activities had death rates two and a half times lower than those who didn't. What's more, these results were independent of the men's age.

A provocative study taking an opposite tack was led by psychologist Larry Scherwitz, Ph.D., of the University of California in San Francisco. Scherwitz and his colleagues were looking at *self-involvement*—in other words, an egocentric focus on the self rather than others—among 577 men in the Multiple Risk Factor Intervention Trial. To measure self-involvement, researchers checked the taped interviews that had been conducted when the subjects first entered the study and counted the number of uses of the words "I," "me," "my," and "mine." Then they compared subjects who had gone on to develop coronary heart disease within about seven years to those with similar risk factors who had not. The researchers found that the ones who became sick did indeed refer to themselves more often in the interviews.

There are some problems with this finding—most notably, the fact that Scherwitz and his fellow researchers failed to replicate the result in a second study using a different set of subject interviews. Nevertheless, given other data on the importance of social involvement and altruism to health, Scherwitz's original finding remains intriguing.

A Friend for Life

Befriending another person may be the ultimate act of selfish selflessness. As described earlier in this book, there is now a substantial literature on the health benefits of having a strong social network. This is seen, for example, in the January/February 1995 issue of the journal *Psychosomatic Medicine*, which opens with an editorial and four research papers devoted to the issue of social support.

In the second of these papers, a researcher from Cornell University Medical College in New York City and his associates studied 26 young women, all students attending a college summer

Self-help groups can help alleviate social isolation for many people.

program. These women were asked to play a video game while their blood pressure and heart rate were continuously monitored. Part of the time, they played the game alone, while the rest of the time, a roommate was present. The roommates had just met the subjects, since they were all new to the area. In addition, the roommates were told not to talk to or touch the subjects. Nevertheless, just having a roommate there to sit nearby and lend silent support seemed to make a difference. Both the subjects' blood pressure readings and their subjective stress ratings were lower under that condition than when they were by themselves.

In the last couple of decades, the search for friends with common interests and concerns has led to the proliferation of *self-help groups.* Such organizations, run by and for their members, are really better described as mutual aid groups. Currently, there are over 4,000 self-help groups operating in New Jersey alone. These organizations can help alleviate the social isolation that people with serious medical conditions or other problems often feel. They can also provide an opportunity for people to share the kind of knowledge that is learned through experience. In addition, many organizations become powerful advocates for the needs and rights of their members.

Self-help groups differ from the kinds of support groups described in the last chapter in that they're run by untrained members rather than professional therapists. In some cases, though, the type of homespun help they offer may be inadequate or even ill-advised. After all, counseling is a difficult and delicate process, even for those with specialized training and considerable experience. It's always possible for abuses to arise, so care should be taken in choosing a self-help group.

A Friend Indeed

One researcher who has examined social ties in older adults is Teresa Seeman, Ph.D., now an associate professor of gerontology at the Andrus Gerontology Center of the University of Southern California. "My interest is in how factors such as a person's degree of social integration and the size of his or her social network influence variables such as physical and cognitive functioning," Seeman says.

A fascinating aspect of her work has been defining just what kinds of relationships truly qualify as supportive. One study included 2,806 people

Having a close friend in whom to confide is important for people of all ages.

aged 65 and older, none of whom were living in a nursing home. In an hour-long interview, the researchers asked about the subjects' number of social ties with children, other relatives, and friends and the nature of those ties—for example, whether they were local or long-distance. The researchers also assessed two kinds of support: instrumental support, which involves direct assistance with household and other daily tasks, and emotional support, which involves having someone to talk problems over with.

Seeman and her coauthor found that having a confidant was strongly associated with both kinds of support. This could be either a spouse or someone else. However, the critical thing seemed to be having someone to confide in, rather than just being married, which was not related to support in itself. Another finding was that grown children were commonly providers of instrumental support, while close friends and family were typically sources of emotional support. Finally, while the size of a person's network and the geographical proximity of family and friends were linked to the availability of support, they weren't necessarily related to its perceived adequacy. Clearly, there's more to being supportive than simply being around.

Helping Yourself to Health

Until 1981, not a single statewide clearinghouse for self-help groups existed in the United States. That's the year when mental health educator Ed Madara formed one in New Jersey. Today Madara is director of the American Self-Help Clearinghouse, based in Denville, N.J., and more than two dozen other state and regional clearinghouses are scattered around the country.

Madara notes that hundreds of self-help groups spring up each week. Here are his tips for starting a new one:

- **Don't reinvent the wheel.** Find out about similar groups that are already in existence. Then contact those organizations and ask for how-to starter packets or sample materials. If there's a clearinghouse in your area, see what assistance it can provide.
- **Think mutual help from the start.** Put up flyers and send out letters looking for others who are interested in starting—not simply joining—a self-help group. Then share the leadership role and make your group a team effort from the outset.
- **Seek out professional assistance.** Consider soliciting advice or other help from professionals who may be sensitive to your

Man and Woman's Best Friend

Of course, friends come in many shapes and sizes—some don't even walk on two legs. As any pet owner can tell you, animals can be a wonderful source of companionship and comfort. Research on whether they also offer the kinds of physical benefits provided by human friends is mixed. However, several studies have now found a positive link between pets and health, at least for animal lovers.

In one influential 1980 study from the Universities of Pennsylvania and Maryland, researchers looked at the survival rate of 92 patients one year after they had been discharged from a coronary care unit. They found that

group's needs. They can be helpful in various ways, including making referrals, offering ideas, and locating useful resources.

- **Choose a meeting time and place.** Try to obtain a free meeting space from a church, community center, hospital, library, or the like. If

Self-help, or mutual aid, groups have proliferated over the last few decades

you expect a small group, it may be possible to hold meetings in the members' homes. It's easier for people to remember the meeting time if it's the same day every month or week.

- **Reach out to potential members.** Let people know about your first regular meeting by contacting interested professionals, posting notices, and placing announcements in the community calendar section of the local newspaper. Allow ample time at the meeting to voice your interests and to hear others' concerns.

28 percent of those who did not own pets had died, versus only 6 percent of the pet owners. Of course, pet ownership itself takes some effort, so it might be an indirect measure of health status. To control for this, the authors tried reanalyzing their data after leaving out any dogs, which they reasoned were among the most time- and energy-consuming pets. Even then, the link between pet ownership and survival was significant.

More recently, a 1990 study from the University of California in Los Angeles looked at doctor visits among 938 Medicare recipients enrolled in one health maintenance organization. After controlling for factors such as age and health status, the researcher found that, over the course of a year, those subjects who owned pets reported fewer doctor contacts than those who didn't. This effect was most pronounced among dog owners.

Several recent studies have found a positive link between pets and health.

The author concluded that dogs more than other pets provide companionship and affection that may be important buffers against stress.

Based on such findings, the Delta Society in Renton, Wash., has established a therapeutic Pet Partners program, which is a nationwide registration system for pets and volunteers. Animals in the program must pass health, skills, and aptitude tests, while their owners must complete volunteer training. Once this is done, the Pet Partners visit hospitalized children, disabled adults, and other people with special physical and psychological needs. The Delta Society calls this approach, which assigns animals an integral part in the treatment process of a human patient, *animal-assisted therapy*—as distinguished from pet therapy, which implies treatment for dogs and cats. The society has now registered over 1,600 Pet Partners teams, which visit hospitals, rehabilitation centers, nursing homes, and other sites.

An interesting sidelight is the observation that man may be dog's best friend, just as surely as the reverse is true. One author of the 1980 study described above was psychologist James Lynch, Ph.D., who also wrote a pioneering popular account of modern mind-body research, a 1977 book titled *The Broken Heart: The Medical Consequences of Loneliness*. In that book, Lynch outlines the evidence for profound cardiovascular changes in animals while being petted by humans.

Music Has Charms to Soothe

Another of life's great pleasures is music, which since ancient times has been associated with medicine. In fact, the Kahum papyrus, the earliest known written record of medical practices, mentions the use of incantations. By the end of the nineteenth century, scientists had begun to study the effects of music on physiological processes such as cardiac output, respiratory rate, and blood pressure.

A 1986 meta-analysis, published in the *Journal of Music Therapy*, compared the results of 30 studies of music in actual medical or dental treatments. It included all such studies the author could find that were written in English and presented hard data in usable form. Every single study found that at least some music conditions were associated with positive effects, as compared to nonmusic conditions. The most common use of music was to reduce pain or anxiety, and studies that employed music for these purposes generally produced the largest gains. The situation in which music's painkilling potential was most obvious was when the combination of music and anesthesia was compared to anesthesia alone.

Today training in *music therapy*—the field that uses music therapeutically to address physical, psychological, and mental functioning—is offered by more than 70 programs at universities around the United States. The field's largest professional organization, the National Association for Music Therapy, now represents over 5,000 therapists, corporate members, and related groups. Clients include people with a wide variety of conditions, including acquired immunodeficiency syndrome (AIDS), Alzheimer's disease, chronic pain, cancer, substance abuse, brain injury, and physical disability.

In the early 1990s, the Administration on Aging of the U.S. Department of Health and Human Services funded six music therapy projects to the tune of $546,000. These music-related projects include a study by therapists in Coral Gables, Fla., of behavior, cognition, and hormones in Alzheimer's disease patients; a study at Duke University Medical Center of physical and psychological effects in patients receiving radiation or physical therapy; and research at Colorado State University on the walking ability of Parkinson's disease patients.

The Music Therapy-Parkinson's Disease Link

The last of those grants went to Michael Thaut, Ph.D., a professor of music therapy and biomedical engineering at Colorado State's Center for Biomedical Research in Music. His project was specifically designed to test the ability of rhythmic music to improve the gait of Parkinson's patients.

Listening to music is often cited as a strategy for coping with pain.

"We're interested in how the auditory and motor systems work together in the control of movement," Thaut says. "We've observed that people have very accurate time coupling to rhythmic beats, and we've tried to make use of this phenomenon with people who have deficits in their movement to see if we can help them relearn to coordinate their walking patterns." Preliminary results presented at the 1995 meeting of the American Neurological Association indicate that Parkinson's patients who practiced walking at home to audiotapes of rhythmic music did improve their gait, compared to subjects who practiced without the tapes or not at all.

In an earlier study with 24 healthy young women, Thaut and his colleagues measured changes in the electrical activity in their upper arm muscles using electromyographic (EMG) sensors. After the sensors were attached to the biceps and triceps of one arm, the volunteers were asked to hit three pads in a particular sequence with their fists. First they did this following their own internal tempo, keeping the beats as even as possible. Then they repeated the process, but this time some of the subjects were given external tempo cues, in the form of a synthesized bass drum sound played at either the subject's natural speed or at a slower speed.

The researchers found that adding the drum rhythm had a marked influence on EMG patterns. For example, there was a decrease in the variation of muscular activity that seemed to indicate more efficient muscle use. It was this kind of observation that led Thaut to speculate that the use of rhythmic music with people such as stroke victims and Parkinson's patients might improve the recovery of motor control and skill, thanks to better anticipation and timing of muscular effort.

The Music Therapy-Pain Link

Music also seems to strike the right chord when it comes to pain control. One researcher who has attempted to quantify this effect is Beverly Whipple, Ph.D., R.N., an associate professor of nursing at Rutgers, The State University of New Jersey. "We've found that music does elevate pain thresholds," Whipple says, "and the mechanism that it works by depends upon the type of music you use."

In a 1992 study of 10 healthy women, Whipple and a colleague tested the effects of different kinds of music on their pain and touch thresholds that is the points at which they were just able to perceive pain and touch. Pain detection thresholds were measured by using sensitive instruments that gradually increased the amount of pressure or heat applied to a hand, while touch detection thresholds were measured by applying a series of nylon filaments of graded stiffness. The reseachers found that soothing music—for example, Pachelbel's Canon in D for Strings and Continuo—raised the women's threshold for pain but not touch. Stimulating music—the second movement of Beethoven's Symphony No. 9 in D minor—raised both. Whipple explains this discrepancy in blocking pain by suggesting that "the soothing music worked as an analgesic," while "the stimulating music worked mainly by distraction."

In fact, distraction—like relaxation, meditation, hypnosis, biofeedback, and imagery—is often mentioned as a pain-coping strategy. Many people instinctively use *distraction,* which involves taking attention away from the pain. For instance, they may listen to music or watch a movie to take their mind off the discomfort. Distraction seems to work particularly well if the pain is sudden and intense or if it is brief, lasting 45 minutes or less. In addition, distraction can be helpful while you're waiting for medication to take effect. Any activity that keeps your mind busy can be tried, whether it's reading, TV watching, needlework, model building, or listening to a particularly rousing passage of music.

The Art of Healthy Living

The age-old connection between the creative arts and the healing arts has led to the rise of yet another field: *art therapy.* The therapeutic use of art in health care settings is intended mainly to help clients resolve emotional conflicts, improve self-awareness, and express unspoken and frequently unconscious concerns. It may be particularly valuable with young children and disabled individuals who are unable to talk about their most pressing and painful worries.

This professional specialty was formalized in 1969, with the founding of the American Art Therapy Association. Today the association represents approximately 4,750 art therapists and students. In a 1992–93 survey by the association, members reported specializing primarily in psychiatric and other psychotherapeutic work. However, among the other specialty areas listed were addiction, aging, Alzheimer's disease, AIDS, chronic illness, and physical disability.

Most research on art therapy has dealt with its impact on emotional and mental health. Unfortunately, there's a dearth of hard data on the use of art to enhance recovery from physical disease. Nevertheless, several hospitals have recently tried integrating art into their regular services. At Shands Hospital at the University of Florida in Gainesville, for example, a well-received Arts in Medicine pilot program was established on the bone marrow transplant unit in 1992. Patients, whose stays averaged six weeks, were given a journal and a stocked art bin, filled with such supplies as colored pencils, markers, crayons, fabric paint, clay, glue, and scissors. In addition, visiting artists worked with the patients and provided workshops for families and staff. In a 1994 article in *Cancer Nursing*, the project's founders note that the fact that the program has spread to other units underscores its value.

It Only Hurts When I Don't Laugh

Another idea that dates back to ancient times is the notion that laughter is linked to healthiness as well as happiness. Modern interest in this idea was revived in 1979, when former *Saturday Review* editor Norman Cousins published his best-selling book *Anatomy of an Illness as Perceived by the Patient: Reflections on Healing and Regeneration*. In the book, Cousins recounts his unexpected recovery from a disabling form of arthritis known as ankylosing spondylitis. He attributes his remarkable turnaround, in part, to self-prescribed doses of belly laughs.

Cousins requested for his hospital room a movie projector, on which he showed episodes of the TV show *Candid Camera* and Marx Brothers films. He also convinced the nurses to read to him from humor books. He discovered that hearty laughter had a pain-killing effect that lasted for at least two hours. Cousins's doctor began checking his blood sedimentation rate, a measure of inflammation, before and after humor episodes and found that it dropped slightly each time.

Physicians were uncertain whether to take Cousins's claims seriously or, fittingly enough, laugh them off. The first chapter of his book had originally appeared three years earlier in the *New England Journal of Medicine*. After that publication, Cousins reported that he received some

3,000 letters from doctors—letters filled with "encouraging support." He was also offered faculty positions at five medical schools, and he eventually served as an adjunct professor at the University of California in Los Angeles until his death in 1990. Yet Cousins's account also drew sharp criticism from some quarters. For example, in 1981 article in *Science*, a sociologist branded his story "illogical" and "self-serving." Among the sociologist's charges: that Cousin's diagnosis was not as definite nor his prognosis as bleak as portrayed. It was also noted that Cousin's account did not conform to standards of scientific evidence. It is only as controlled research has begun to substantiate a link between mirth and health that Cousins has been at least partially vindicated.

He Who Laughs, Lasts

Data or no, the chuckle-a-day prescription has undeniable charms. This helps explain why so many medical centers around the country have implemented *humor programs*. Among the approaches that have been tried are humor libraries and comedy carts, which let hospitalized patients select humor materials in their rooms. A sampling of the facilities involved includes Morton Plant Hospital in Clearwater, Fla.; the Medical Center of Vermont in Burlington; Riverview Cancer Care Medical Associates in Rexford, N.Y.; the Veterans Administration Hospital in Buffalo, N.Y.; and the University of New Mexico Hospital in Albuquerque.

There are other signs that humor is gaining therapeutic credibility. One example is a California-based conference on the Healing Power of Laughter & Play, which has been held every few years since 1982. Its 1995 meeting in San Francisco attracted more than 500 therapists, counselors, doctors, nurses, and laypersons. Continuing education credits were even offered to the professionals in the crowd.

Another example is the Humor Project, an organization in Saratoga Springs, N.Y., whose stated aim is to help people and organizations tap into the positive power of humor and creativity. Founder and president Joel Goodman, Ed.D., is now much in demand as a speaker, writer, and consultant. Even the normally staid *Journal of the American Medical Association* recently featured an essay by Goodman on "taking your job seriously and yourself lightly." Among the topics discussed at the Humor

Watching a funny movie may lead to increases in activated T cells, natural killer cells, and B cells.

Project's annual conference in 1995 were current and future applications of humor in health care, the art and psychology of positive humor, and "the worth of mirth."

Stanford psychiatrist William Fry, M.D., has documented a number of physiological changes associated with laughter and mirth, involving the muscular, respiratory, cardiovascular, endocrine, immune, and nervous systems. He notes that, while laughter initially has a stimulating effect, after it subsides, a brief period of relaxation ensues. During boisterous laughter, many muscles are activated, providing a sort of internal work-out that may be especially beneficial to people who are bedridden or wheelchair-bound. Conversely, the relaxation that follows laughter eases muscle tension, which may help break the spasm-pain cycle experienced by many neuralgia, or nerve pain, and arthritis patients.

The Humor-Immune System Link

Of particular interest is the salutary effect laughter may have on the immune system. One of the foremost researchers in this area is Lee Berk, Dr.P.H., an assistant professor of preventive medicine at the Loma Linda University School of Medicine in California. Berk studies *eustress,* healthy stress that may accompany positive emotional states. "Eustress," he says, "is really the reciprocal of distress."

In a paper presented at the 1995 meeting of the Society of Behavioral Medicine, Berk and his coauthor looked at the production of a type of virus-fighting interferon by the white blood cells. The study included a small group of healthy men who watched a 60-minute humor video. Blood samples were taken before, during, and after the viewing and the next day. The researchers found that the men's interferon level rose, compared to what it had been before the video began, and stayed higher for at least a day. In earlier papers, the researchers had already described other immune changes in subjects who had been exposed to humor, including increases in activated T cells, natural killer cells, B cells, and *immunoglobulins,* the family of proteins that includes antibodies.

Berk and his colleagues had also previously found a number of neuroendocrine and stress hormone changes associated with what he calls "mirthful laughter." In a 1989 study with a similar design, they showed, among other things, that blood levels of epinephrine and *cortisol,* one of the glucocorticoid hormones released as part of the classic stress response, decreased after watching a humor video.

Berk calls the study of laughter-related immune and endocrine effects "the frontier of frontiers." He adds, "It's exciting to discover that eustress modulates these immune system components. It must be of some consequence after all."

For Thrill-Seekers Only

If laughter and joy really do promote better health, then the sound of a joke or the sight of a sunset should be tonics for what ails us. In fact, there is scientific evidence that this is so. Among the findings of the Tecumseh study by House, described earlier in this chapter, was a lower death rate in men who went on pleasure drives and picnics or attended cultural and sporting events.

If you're looking for a guide to what may deliver that quick rush of pleasure, science can even help there. An often-cited 1980 study by Stanford pharmacology professor Avram Goldstein, Ph.D., investigated the kinds of stimuli that give folks a thrill—what the dictionary defines as "a subtle nervous tremor caused by intense emotion or excitement . . . , producing a slight shudder or tingling through the body."

Goldstein sent questionnaires to employees of an addiction research foundation where he worked and to medical and music students at Stanford. Although this was far from a random sample, the responses are interesting. Among the music students, the only group to receive a structured checklist, the stimuli rated as sometimes causing a thrill by at least two-thirds of the respondents included:

- musical passages—not a surprising finding for music students, of course, but also frequently mentioned by the scientists and medical students
- scenes in a movie, play, ballet, or book
- great beauty in nature or art
- physical contact with another person
- climactic moments in opera
- nostalgic moments
- sexual activity
- viewing a beautiful painting, photograph, or sculpture
- watching emotional interactions between other people.

If you think many of these points sound familiar, you're right. The emphasis on music, art, social contact, and emotional expression echoes therapeutic themes discussed in the previous pages. Goldstein's primary aim in collecting these data was to study endorphins: Once he knew that music often elicits a thrill, he gave 10 subjects a drug that blocked the body's natural opiates and found that it also diminished the musical thrills for some of them.

It seems, then, that the human brain is equipped with chemicals designed to make us shiver with delight at the very things that promote well-being. Thus, in Goldstein's study, we catch a glimpse of nature's mechanism for letting us know how to nurture our own good health.

General References

Borysenko, J. *Minding the Body, Mending the Mind.* New York: Bantam, 1987.

Goleman, D., and J. Gurin, eds. *Mind/Body Medicine: How to Use Your Mind for Better Health.* Yonkers, N.Y.: Consumer Reports, 1993.

Institute of Noetic Sciences. *The Heart of Healing.* Atlanta: Turner, 1993.

Locke, S., and D. Colligan *The Healer Within: The New Medicine of Mind and Body.* New York: Mentor, 1986.

Moyers, B. *Healing and the Mind.* New York: Doubleday, 1993.

Office of Alternative Medicine. *Alternative Medicine: Expanding Medical Horizons.* U.S. Government Printing Office, Washington, D.C.: NIH Publication No. 94–066, 1994.

Ornstein, R., and D. Sobel. *The Healing Brain: Breakthrough Discoveries About How the Brain Keeps Us Healthy.* New York: Simon and Schuster, 1987.

Pelletier, K.R. *Mind as Healer, Mind as Slayer: A Holistic Approach to Preventing Stress Disorders.* New York: Delta, 1977.

Chapter 1. Mind-Body Medicine

Alexander, F. "Psychological Aspects of Medicine." *Psychosomatic Medicine* 1 (1939): 7–18.

Eisenberg, D.M., R.C. Kessler, C. Foster, F.E. Norlock, D.R. Calkins, and T.L. Delbanco. "Unconventional Medicine in the United States: Prevalence, Costs, and Patterns of Use." *New England Journal of Medicine* 328 (1993): 246–252.

Gordon, J.S. *The Healing Partnership: Essays for Health Professionals, Students, and Patients.* Washington, D.C.: Aurora Associates, 1984.

Greenfield, S., S. Kaplan, and J.E. Ware. "Expanding Patient Involvement in Care: Effects on Patient Outcomes." *Annals of Internal Medicine* 102 (1985): 520–528.

Jones, L. "On a Front Line." *British Medical Journal* 310 (1995): 1052-1054.

Moore, N., and H. Komras. *Patient-Focused Healing: Integrating Caring and Curing in Health Care.* San Francisco: Jossey-Bass, 1993.

Smith, R.C., J.S. Lyles, J.A. Mettler, A.A. Marshall, L.F. VanEgeren, B.E. Stoffelmayr, G.G. Osborn, and V. Shebroe. "Improved Patient Satisfaction from Training Residents in Psychosocial Medicine" (abstract). *Psychosomatic Medicine* 57 (1995): 69.

Ulrich, R.S. "View Through a Window May Influence Recovery from Surgery." *Science* 224 (1984): 420–421.

Voelker, R. "New Trends Aimed at Healing by Design." *Journal of the American Medical Association* 272 (1994): 1885–1886.

Chapter 2. All in Your Mind: Emotions, Beliefs, and Health

Barefoot, J.C., B.L. Peterson, F.E. Harrell, M.A. Hlatky, D.B.

Pryor, T.L. Haney, J.A. Blumenthal, I.C. Siegler, and R.B. Williams. "Type A Behavior and Survival: A Follow-Up Study of 1,467 Patients with Coronary Artery Disease." *American Journal of Cardiology* 64 (1989): 427–432.

Berkman, L.F., and L. Syme. "Social Networks, Host Resistance, and Mortality: A Nine-Year Follow-Up Study of Alameda County Residents." *American Journal of Epidemiology* 109 (1979): 186–204.

Braun, B.G. "Psychophysiologic Phenomena in Multiple Personality and Hypnosis." *American Journal of Clinical Hypnosis* 26 (1983): 124–137.

Cassileth, B.R., E.J. Lusk, D.S. Miller, L.L. Brown, and C. Miller. "Psychosocial Correlates of Survival in Advanced Malignant Disease?" *New England Journal of Medicine* 312 (1985): 1551–1555.

Cole, S.W., M.E. Kemeny, S.E. Taylor, and B.R. Visscher. "Rejection-Sensitivity Mediates Accelerated Course of HIV Infection in Gay Men Who Conceal Their Homosexuality" (abstract). *Psychosomatic Medicine* 57 (1995): 72.

Curtin, S.G., O.E. Walton, J.C. Barefoot, B. Fredrickson, M.J. Helms, C.M. Kuhn, E.C. Suarez, and R.B. Williams. "Violence in the Media: Effects of Affective Response, Gender and Hostility of the Viewer Upon Neuroendocrine Reactivity" (abstract). *Psychosomatic Medicine* 57 (1995): 73.

Frasure-Smith, N., F. Lespérance, and M. Talajic. "Depression and 18-Month Prognosis After Myocardial Infarction." *Circulation* 91 (1995): 999–1005.

Friedman, M., and R.H. Rosenman. *Type A Behavior and Your Heart.* New York, Fawcett Crest, 1974.

Futterman, A.D., M.E. Kemeny, D. Shapiro, and J.L. Fahey. "Immunological and Physiological Changes Associated with Induced Positive and Negative Mood." *Psychosomatic Medicine* 56 (1994): 499–511.

Hall, N.R.S., M. O'Grady, and D. Calandra. "Transformation of Personality and the Immune System." *Advances* 10 (1994): 7–15.

Kneier, A.W., and L. Temoshok. "Repressive Coping Reactions in Patients with Malignant Melanoma as Compared to Cardiovascular Disease Patients." *Journal of Psychosomatic Research* 28 (1984): 145–155.

Leor, J., and R.A. Kloner. "The January 17, 1994 Los Angeles Earthquake as a Trigger for Acute Myocardial Infarction" (abstract). *Journal of the American College of Cardiology* Suppl. (1995): 105A.

Levin, J.S., and H.Y. Vanderpool. "Is Religion Therapeutically Significant for Hypertension?" *Social Science and Medicine* 29 (1989): 69–78.

Maddi, S.R., and S.C. Kobasa. *The Hardy Executive: Health Under Stress.* Homewood, Ill.: Dow Jones-Irwin, 1984.

McCraty, R., M. Atkinson, W.A. Tiller, and G. Rein. "Autonomic Assessment Using Power Spectral Analysis of Heart Rate Variability in Emotional States" (abstract). *Psychosomatic Medicine* 57 (1995): 84.

Mittleman, M.A., M. Maclure, J.B. Sherwood, R.P. Mulry, G.H. Tofler, S.C. Jacobs, R. Friedman, H. Benson, and J.E. Muller. "Triggering of Acute Myocardial Infarction Onset by Episodes of Anger." *Circulation* 92 (1995): 1720-1725.

Morris, P.L.P., R.G. Robinson, P. Andrzejewski, J. Samuels, and T.R. Price. "Association of Depression with 10-Year Poststroke Mortality." *American Journal of Psychiatry* 150 (1993): 124–129.

Peterson, C., M.E.P. Seligman, and G.E. Vaillant. "Pessimistic Explanatory Style Is a Risk Factor for Physical Illness: A Thirty-Five-Year Longitudinal Study." *Journal of Personality and Social Psychology* 55 (1988): 23–27.

Phillips, D.P., and D.G. Smith. "Postponement of Death Until Symbolically Meaningful Occasions." *Journal of the American Medical Association* 263 (1990): 1947–1951.

Ragland, D.R., and R.J. Brand. "Type A Behavior and Mortality from Coronary Heart Disease." *New England Journal of Medicine* 318 (1988): 65–69.

Rodin, J., and E.J. Langer. "Long-Term Effects of a Control-Relevant Intervention with the Institutionalized Aged." *Journal of Personality and Social Psychology* 35 (1977): 897–902.

Rosenman, R.H., R.J. Brand, C.D. Jenkins, M. Friedman, R. Straus, and M. Wurm. "Coronary Heart Disease in the Western Collaborative Group Study: Final Follow-Up Experience of 8½ Years." *Journal of the American Medical Association* 233 (1975): 872–877.

Seligman, M.E.P. *Learned Optimism: How to Change Your Mind and Your Life.* New York: Pocket, 1990.

Shekelle, R.B., S.B. Hulley, J.D. Neaton, J.H. Billings, N.O. Borhani, T.A. Gerace, D.R. Jacobs, N.L. Lasser, M.B. Mittlemark, and J. Stamler. "The MRFIT Behavior Pattern Study: II. Type A Behavior and Incidence of Coronary Heart Disease." *American Journal of Epidemiology* 122 (1985): 559–570.

Solomon, G.F., D. Benton, J.O. Harker, B. Bonavida, and M.A. Fletcher. "Prolonged Asymptomatic States in HIV-Seropositive Persons with Fewer Than 50 CD4+ T Cells per MM^3: Psychoneuroimmunologic Findings." *Annals of the New York Academy of Sciences* 741 (1994): 185–190.

Temoshok, L., and H. Dreher. *The Type C Connection: The Mind-Body Link to Cancer and Your Health.* New York: Plume, 1992.

Visintainer, M.A., J.R. Volpicelli, and M.E.P. Seligman. "Tumor Rejection in Rats After Inescapable or Escapable Shock." *Science* 216 (1982): 437–439.

Williams, R., and V. Williams. *Anger Kills: Seventeen Strategies for Controlling the Hostility That Can Harm Your Health.* New York: HarperPerennial, 1993.

Williams, R.B., J.C. Barefoot, R.M. Califf, T.L. Haney, W.B. Saunders, D.B. Pryor, M.A. Hlatky, I.C. Siegler, and D.B. Mark. "Prognostic Importance of Social and Economic Resources Among Medically Treated Patients with Angiographically Documented Coronary Artery Disease." *Journal of the American Medical Association* 267 (1992): 520–524.

Williams, R.B., T.L. Haney, K.L. Lee, Y.-H. Kong, J.A. Blumenthal, and R.E. Whalen. "Type A Behavior, Hostility, and Coronary Atherosclerosis." *Psychosomatic Medicine* 42 (1980): 539–549.

Chapter 3. Minding the Body: Psychoneuroimmunology

Ader, R. "Behaviorally Conditioned Immunosuppression" (letter). *Psychosomatic Medicine* 36 (1974): 183–184.

Ader, R., and N. Cohen. "Behaviorally Conditioned Immunosuppression." *Psychosomatic Medicine* 37 (1975): 333–340.

Ader, R., D.L. Felten, and N. Cohen, eds. *Psychoneuroimmunology,* 2nd ed. San Diego: Academic, 1991.

Besedovsky, H., E. Sorkin, D. Felix, and H. Haas. "Hypothalamic Changes During the Immune Response." *European Journal of Immunology* 7 (1977): 323–325.

Blalock, J.E. "The Immune System as a Sensory Organ." *Journal of Immunology* 132 (1984): 1067–70.

Blalock, J.E., and J.D. Stanton. "Common Pathways of Interferon and Hormonal Action." *Nature* 283 (1980): 406–408.

Cohen, S., D.A.J. Tyrrell, and A.P. Smith. "Psychological Stress and Susceptibility to the Common Cold." *New England Journal of Medicine* 325 (1991): 606–612.

Felten, D.L., and S.Y. Felten. "Sympathetic Noradrenergic Innervation of Immune Organs." *Brain, Behavior, and Immunity* 2 (1988): 293–300.

Jerne, N.K. "The Generative Grammar of the Immune System." *Science* 229 (1985): 1057–1059.

Kiecolt-Glaser, J.K., J.R. Dura, C.E. Speicher, O.J. Trask, and R. Glaser. "Spousal Caregivers of Dementia Victims: Longitudinal Changes in Immunity and Health." *Psychosomatic Medicine* 53 (1991): 345–362.

Kiecolt-Glaser, J.K., W. Garner, C. Speicher, G.M. Penn, J. Holliday, and R. Glaser. "Psychosocial Modifiers of Immunocompetence in Medical Students." *Psychosomatic Medicine* 46 (1984): 7–14.

Nossal, G.J.V. "Life, Death and the Immune System." *Scientific American* 269 (1993): 21–28, 30.

Olness, K., and R. Ader. "Conditioning as an Adjunct in the Pharmacotherapy of Lupus Erythematosus." *Journal of Developmental and Behavioral Pediatrics* 13 (1992): 124–125.

Pert, C.B., M.R. Ruff, R.J. Weber, and M. Herkenham. "Neuropeptides and Their Receptors: A Psychosomatic Network." *Journal of Immunology* 135 (1985): 820S-826S.

Pert, C.B., and S.H. Snyder. "Opiate Receptor: Demonstration in Nervous Tissue." *Science* 179 (1973): 1011–1014.

Renoux, G., K. Biziere, M. Renoux, and J.M. Guillaumin. "The Production of T-Cell-Inducing Factors in Mice Is Controlled by the Brain Neocortex." *Scandinavian Journal of Immunology* 17 (1983): 45–50.

Smith, E.M., and J.E. Blalock. "Human Lymphocyte Production of Corticotropin and Endorphin-like Substances: Association with Leukocyte Interferon." *Proceedings of the National Academy of Sciences, USA* 78 (1981): 7530–7534.

Solomon, G.F. *Postulates and Their Evidence Concerning Similarities and Communication Between the Immune System and the Nervous System. Three Decades of Exponential Growth of Psychoneuroimmunology.* San Francisco: Fund for Psychoneuroimmunology, 1994.

Sternberg, E.M., G.P. Chrousos, R.L. Wilder, and P.W. Gold. "The Stress Response and the Regulation of Inflammatory Disease." *Annals of Internal Medicine* 117 (1992): 854–866.

Williams, J.M., R.G. Peterson, P.A. Shea, J.F. Schmedtje, D.C. Bauer, and D.L. Felten. "Sympathetic Innervation of Murine

Thymus and Spleen: Evidence for a Functional Link Between the Nervous and Immune Systems." *Brain Research Bulletin* 6 (1981): 83–94.

Chapter 4. Stress and Dis-stress: The Relaxation Response

Benson, H. *The Relaxation Response.* New York: Avon, 1975.

Bernard, C. *An Introduction to the Study of Experimental Medicine.* New York: Macmillan, 1927.

Cannon, W.B. " 'Voodoo' Death." *Psychosomatic Medicine* 19 (1957): 182–190.

Cannon, W.B. *The Wisdom of the Body.* New York: W.W. Norton, 1960.

Dillon, K.M. "Popping Sealed Air-Capsules to Reduce Stress." *Psychological Reports* 71 (1992): 243–246.

Dossey, L. *Healing Words: The Power of Prayer and the Practice of Medicine.* San Francisco: Harper, 1993.

Friedman, R., W.C. Siegel, S.C. Jacobs, and H. Benson. "Distress Over the Noneffect of Stress" (letter). *Journal of the American Medical Association* 268 (1992): 198.

Gardner, L.I. "Deprivation Dwarfism." *Scientific American* 227 (1972): 76–82.

Hoffman, J.W., H. Benson, P.A. Arns, G.L. Stainbrook, L. Landsberg, J.B. Young, and A. Gill. "Reduced Sympathetic Nervous System Responsivity Associated with the Relaxation Response." *Science* 215 (1982): 190–192.

King, D.E., and B. Bushwick. "Beliefs and Attitudes of Hospital Inpatients About Faith Healing and Prayer." *Journal of Family Practice* 39 (1994): 349–352.

Klinnert, M.D., P.J. Mrazek, and D.A. Mrazek. "Early Asthma Onset: The Interaction Between Family Stressors and Adaptive Parenting." *Psychiatry* 57 (1994): 51–61.

Marwick, C. "Should Physicians Prescribe Prayer for Health? Spiritual Aspects of Well-Being Considered." *Journal of the American Medical Association* 273 (1995): 1561–1562.

Mills, P.J., J.E. Dimsdale, M.G. Ziegler, and R.A. Nelesen. "Racial Differences in Epinephrine and β_2-Adrenergic Receptors." *Hypertension* 25 (1995): 88–91.

Nelesen, R.A., J.E. Dimsdale, P.J. Mills, and M.G. Ziegler. "Relationship of Insulin, Race, and Hypertension with Hemodynamic Reactivity to a Behavioral Challenge." *American Journal of Hypertension* 8 (1995): 12–19.

Sapolsky, R.M. "Stress in the Wild." *Scientific American* 262 (1990): 116–123.

Sapolsky, R.M. *Why Zebras Don't Get Ulcers: A Guide to Stress, Stress-Related Diseases, and Coping.* New York: W.H. Freeman, 1994.

Schor, J.B. *The Overworked American: The Unexpected Decline of Leisure.* New York: BasicBooks, 1991.

Selye, H. *The Stress of Life.* New York: McGraw-Hill, 1976.

Stabler, B., M.E. Tancer, L.M. Nicholas, J. Ranc, and L.E. Underwood. "Social Phobia in Adults Who Were Short During Childhood" (abstract). *Psychosomatic Medicine* 57 (1995): 91.

Trials of Hypertension Prevention Collaborative Research Group. "The Effects of Nonpharmacologic Interventions on Blood Pressure of Persons with High Normal Levels: Results of the Trials of Hypertension Prevention, Phase I." *Journal of the American Medical Association* 267 (1992): 1213–1220.

Wallace, R.K., H. Benson, and A.F. Wilson. "A Wakeful Hypometabolic Physiologic State." *American Journal of Physiology* 221 (1971): 795–799.

Chapter 5. Mind on the Mend: Meditation, Hypnosis, and Biofeedback

Barber, T.X., N.P. Spanos, and J.F. Chaves. *Hypnosis, Imagination, and Human Potentialities.* New York: Pergamon, 1974.

Carlson, C.R., and R.H. Hoyle. "Efficacy of Abbreviated Progressive Muscle Relaxation Training: A Quantitative Review of Behavioral Medicine Research." *Journal of Consulting and Clinical Psychology* 61 (1993): 1059–1067.

Cohn, V. *News & Numbers: A Guide to Reporting Statistical Claims and Controversies in Health and Other Fields.* Ames: Iowa State University, 1989.

Disbrow, E.A., H.L. Bennett, and J.T. Owings. "Effect of Preoperative Suggestion on Postoperative Gastrointestinal

Motility." *Western Journal of Medicine* 158 (1993): 488–492.

Erickson, M.H. "The Interspersal Hypnotic Technique for Symptom Correction and Pain Control." *American Journal of Clinical Hypnosis* 8 (1966): 198–209.

Ewin, D.M. "Delayed Response to Hypnosis?" *American Journal of Clinical Hypnosis* 32 (1989): 142–143.

Ewin, D.M. "Hypnotherapy for Warts (Verruca Vulgaris): 41 Consecutive Cases with 33 Cures." *American Journal of Clinical Hypnosis* 35 (1992): 1–10.

Fawzy, F.I., N.W. Fawzy, L.A. Arndt, and R.O. Pasnau. "Critical Review of Psychosocial Interventions in Cancer Care." *Archives of General Psychiatry* 52 (1995): 100–113.

Jacobson, E. *You Must Relax.* New York: McGraw-Hill, 1976.

Kabat-Zinn, J. *Full Catastrophe Living: Using the Wisdom of Your Body and Mind to Face Stress, Pain, and Illness.* New York: Delta, 1990.

Klopfer, B. "Psychological Variables in Human Cancer." *Journal of Projective Techniques* 21 (1957): 331–340.

Massion, A.O., J. Teas, J.R. Herbert, M.D. Wertheimer, and J. Kabat-Zinn. "Meditation, Melatonin and Breast/Prostate Cancer: Hypothesis and Preliminary Data." *Medical Hypotheses* 44 (1995): 39–46.

McGrady, A., B.K. Bailey, and M.P. Good. "Controlled Study of Biofeedback-Assisted Relaxation in Type I Diabetes." *Diabetes Care* 14 (1991): 360–365.

McGrady, A., and L. Gerstenmaier. "Effect of Biofeedback Assisted Relaxation Training on Blood Glucose Levels in a Type I Insulin Dependent Diabetic: A Case Report." *Journal of Behavior Therapy and Experimental Psychiatry* 21 (1990): 69–75.

Mehl, L.E. "Hypnosis and Conversion of the Breech to the Vertex Presentation." *Archives of Family Medicine* 3 (1994): 881–887.

Olness, K., J.T. MacDonald, and D.L. Uden. "Comparison of Self-Hypnosis and Propranolol in the Treatment of Juvenile Classic Migraine." *Pediatrics* 79 (1987): 593–597.

Orme-Johnson, D. "Medical Care Utilization and the Transcendental Meditation Program." *Psychosomatic Medicine* 49 (1987): 493–507.

Pallak, M.S., N.A. Cummings, H. Dorken, and C.J. Henke. "Effect of Mental Health Treatment on Medical Costs." *Mind/Body Medicine* 1 (1995): 7–12.

Rausch, V. "Cholecystectomy with Self-Hypnosis." *American Journal of Clinical Hypnosis* 22 (1980): 124–129.

Roberts, A.H., D.G. Kewman, L. Mercier, and M. Hovell. "The Power of Nonspecific Effects in Healing: Implications for Psychosocial and Biological Treatments." *Clinical Psychology Review* 13 (1993): 375–391.

Schultz, J.H. *Autogenic Methods.* New York: Grune & Stratton, 1969.

Skolnick, A.A. "Maharishi Ayur-Veda: Guru's Marketing Scheme Promises the World Eternal 'Perfect Health.'" *Journal of the American Medical Association* 266 (1991): 1741–1750.

Spanos, N.P., V. Williams, and M.I. Gwynn. "Effects of Hypnotic, Placebo, and Salicylic Acid Treatments on Wart Regression." *Psychosomatic Medicine* 52 (1990): 109–114.

Chapter 6. More Mind Menders: Imagery and Psychotherapy

Achterberg, J., B. Dossey, and L. Kolkmeier. *Rituals of Healing: Using Imagery for Health and Wellness.* New York: Bantam, 1994.

Antoni, M.H., L. Baggett, G. Ironson, A. LaPerriere, S. August, N. Klimas, N. Schneiderman, and M.A. Fletcher. "Cognitive-Behavioral Stress Management Intervention Buffers Distress Responses and Immunologic Changes Following Notification of HIV-1 Seropositivity." *Journal of Consulting and Clinical Psychology* 59 (1991): 906–915.

Beck, A.T., A.J. Rush, B.F. Shaw, and G. Emery. *Cognitive Therapy of Depression.* New York: Guilford, 1979.

Domar, A.D., M.M. Seibel, and H. Benson. "The Mind/Body Program for Infertility: A New Behavioral Treatment Approach for Women with Infertility." *Fertility and Sterility* 53 (1990): 246–249.

Dowling, S.J. "Lourdes Cures and Their Medical Assessment." *Journal of the Royal Society of Medicine* 77 (1984): 634–638.

Engler, J., and D. Goleman. *The Consumer's Guide to Psychotherapy.* New York: Fireside, 1992.

Esterling, B.A., M.H. Antoni, M.A. Fletcher, S. Margulies, and N. Schneiderman. "Emotional Disclosure Through Writing or Speaking Modulates Latent Epstein-Barr Virus Antibody Titers." *Journal of Consulting and Clinical Psychology* 62 (1994): 130–140.

Fawzy, F.I., N.W. Fawzy, C.S. Hyun, R. Elashoff, D. Guthrie, J.L. Fahey, and D.L. Morton. "Malignant Melanoma: Effects of an Early Structured Psychiatric Intervention, Coping, and Affective State on Recurrence and Survival 6 Years Later." *Archives of General Psychiatry* 50 (1993): 681–689.

Gellert, G.A., R.M. Maxwell, and B.S. Siegel. "Survival of Breast Cancer Patients Receiving Adjunctive Psychosocial Support Therapy: A 10-Year Follow-Up Study." *Journal of Clinical Oncology* 11 (1993): 66–69.

Holland, J.C., and J.H. Rowland, eds. *Handbook of Psychoncology: Psychological Care of the Patient with Cancer.* New York: Oxford University, 1989.

Kutz, I., J.Z. Borysenko, and H. Benson. "Meditation and Psychotherapy: A Rationale for the Integration of Dynamic Psychotherapy, the Relaxation Response, and Mindfulness Meditation." *American Journal of Psychiatry* 142 (1985): 1–8.

O'Regan, B. "Healing, Remission and Miracle Cures." Institute of Noetic Sciences, Sausalito, CA: 1987.

Ornish, D. *Dr. Dean Ornish's Program for Reversing Heart Disease.* New York: Ballantine, 1990.

Ornish, D., S.E. Brown, L.W. Scherwitz, J.H. Billings, W.T. Armstrong, T.A. Ports, S.M. McLanahan, R.L. Kirkeeide, R.J. Brand, and K.L. Gould. "Can Lifestyle Changes Reverse Coronary Heart Disease? The Lifestyle Heart Trial." *Lancet* 336 (1990): 129–133.

Pennebaker, J.W. *Opening Up: The Healing Power of Confiding in Others.* New York: William Morrow, 1990.

Sacks, M.H. "Psychiatry and Sport." *Annals of Sports Medicine* 5 (1990): 47–52.

Siegel, B.S. *Love, Medicine & Miracles: Lessons Learned About Self-Healing from a Surgeon's Experience with Exceptional Patients.* New York: Harper-Perennial, 1986.

Simonton, O.C., S. Matthews-Simonton, and J.L. Creighton. *Getting Well Again.* New York: Bantam, 1978.

Spiegel, D. *Living Beyond Limits.* New York: Fawcett Columbine, 1993.

Spiegel, D., J.R. Bloom, H.C. Kraemer, and E. Gottheil. "Effect of Psychosocial Treatment on Survival of Patients with Metastatic Breast Cancer." *Lancet* (1989): 888–891.

Strain, J.J., J.S. Lyons, J.S. Hammer, M. Fahs, A. Lebovits, P.L. Paddison, S. Snyder, E. Strauss, R. Burton, G. Nuber, T. Abernathy, H. Sacks, J. Nordlie, and C. Sacks. "Cost Offset from a Psychiatric Consultation-Liaison

Intervention with Elderly Hip Fracture Patients." *American Journal of Psychiatry* 148 (1991): 1044–1049.

Chapter 7. The Joy of . . . Joy: Friends, Pets, Music, Art, and Humor

Berk, L.S., and S.A. Tan. "Eustress of Mirthful Laughter Modulates the Immune System Lymphokine Interferon-Gamma" (abstract). *Annals of Behavioral Medicine* 17 (1995): S158.

Berk, L.S., S.A. Tan, W.F. Fry, B.J. Napier, J.W. Lee, R.W. Hubbard, J.E. Lewis, and W.C. Eby. "Neuroendocrine and Stress Hormone Changes During Mirthful Laughter." *American Journal of the Medical Sciences* 298 (1989): 390–396.

Cousins, N. "Anatomy of an Illness (as Perceived by the Patient)." *New England Journal of Medicine* 295 (1976): 1458–1463.

Cousins, N. *Anatomy of an Illness as Perceived by the Patient: Reflections on Healing and Regeneration.* New York: Bantam, 1979.

Friedmann, E., A.H. Katcher, J.J. Lynch, and S.A. Thomas. "Animal Companions and One-Year Survival of Patients After Discharge from a Coronary Care Unit." *Public Health Reports* 95 (1980): 307–312.

Fry, W.F. "The Physiologic Effects of Humor, Mirth, and Laughter." *Journal of the American Medical Association* 267 (1992): 1857–1858.

Gerin, W., D. Milner, S. Chawla, and T.G. Pickering. "Social Support as a Moderator of Cardiovascular Reactivity in Women: A Test of the Direct Effects and Buffering Hypotheses." *Psychosomatic Medicine* 57 (1995): 16–22.

Goldstein, A. "Thrills in Response to Music and Other Stimuli." *Physiological Psychology* 8 (1980): 126–129.

Goodman, J.B. "Laughing Matters: Taking Your Job Seriously and Yourself Lightly." *Journal of the American Medical Association* 267 (1992): 1858.

Graham, L.E., L. Scherwitz, and R. Brand. "Self-Reference and Coronary Heart Disease Incidence in the Western Collaborative Group Study." *Psychosomatic Medicine* 51 (1989): 137–144.

Holden, C. "Cousins' Account of Self-Cure Rapped." *Science* 214 (1981): 892.

House, J.S., C. Robbins, and H.L. Metzner. "The Association of Social Relationships and Activities with Mortality: Prospective Evidence from the Tecumseh Community Health

Study." *American Journal of Epidemiology* 116 (1982): 123–140.

Lane, M.T.R., and J. Graham-Pole. "Development of an Art Program on a Bone Marrow Transplant Unit." *Cancer Nursing* 17 (1994): 185–192.

Lynch, J.J. *The Broken Heart: The Medical Consequences of Loneliness.* New York: Basic, 1977.

McIntosh, G.C., M.H. Thaut, R.R. Rice, R.A. Miller, J. Rathbun, and J.M. Brault. "Rhythmic Facilitation in Gait Training of Parkinson's Disease" (abstract). *Annals of Neurology* 38 (1995): 331.

Ornstein, R., and D. Sobel. *Healthy Pleasures.* Reading, Mass.: Addison-Wesley, 1989.

Pelletier, K.R. *Sound Mind, Sound Body: A New Model for Lifelong Health.* Fireside: New York, 1994.

Scherwitz, L., L.E. Graham, G. Grandits, J. Buehler, and J. Billings. "Self-Involvement and Coronary Heart Disease Incidence in the Multiple Risk Factor Intervention Trial." *Psychosomatic Medicine* 48 (1986): 187–199.

Seeman, T.E., and L.F. Berkman. "Structural Characteristics of Social Networks and Their Relationship with Social Support in the Elderly: Who Provides Support." *Social Science and Medicine* 26 (1988): 737–749.

Siegel, J.M. "Stressful Life Events and Use of Physician Services Among the Elderly: The Moderating Role of Pet Ownership." *Journal of Personality and Social Psychology* 58 (1990): 1081–1086.

Standley, J.M. "Music Research in Medical/Dental Treatment: Meta-analysis and Clinical Applications." *Journal of Music Therapy* 23 (1986): 56–122.

Thaut, M., S. Schleiffers, and W. Davis. "Analysis of EMG Activity in Biceps and Triceps Muscle in an Upper Extremity Gross Motor Task Under the Influence of Auditory Rhythm." *Journal of Music Therapy* 28 (1991): 64–88.

Whipple, B., and N.J. Glynn. "Quantification of the Effects of Listening to Music as a Noninvasive Method of Pain Control." *Scholarly Inquiry for Nursing Practice* 6 (1992): 43–62.

P H O T O   C R E D I T S

Photo research: *Christopher Deegan, Beth Krumholz, Laurie Platt Winfrey/Carousel Research*

*Abrreviations: SPL = Science Photo Library, PR = Photo Researchers,
CMSP = Custom Medical Stock Photo*

p.2—© Bonnie Kamin/PhotoEdit
p.3—© CMSP/SPL
p.4—© Yoav Levy/Phototake NYC

CHAPTER 1
*p.11—© Ann Chwatsky/Phototake NYC   p.13—© Photographie BULLOZ, Paris
p.15—© AP/Wide World Photo   p.17—© Courtesy St. Charles Medical Center, Bend, Oregon
p.18—© Courtesy Trinity Medical Center, Moline, Illinois   p.20—© Will and Deni McIntyre/PR
p.21—© Tom McCarthy/PhotoEdit   p.23—© CMSP*

CHAPTER 2
*p.26—© Tate Gallery, London/Art Resource, New York   p.28—© Will and Deni McIntyre/PR
p.31—© Richard Hutchings/PR   p.32—© PhotoEdit   p.34—© CMSP   p.37—© Arthur Tress/PR
p.38—© Sheila Terry, SPL/PR   p.39—© David Young-Wolff/PhotoEdit
p.41—© Richard Hutchings/PR*

CHAPTER 3
*p.47—© CMSP   p.48—© Alfred Pasieka, SPL/PR   p.49—© Microworks/DAN/Phototake NYC
p.50—© Alfred Pasieka, SPL/PR   p.52—© G&H SOHO   p.54—© James Stevenson, SPL/PR
p.55—© David Young-Wolff/PhotoEdit   p.56—© Omikron/PR   p.59—© Alfred Pasieka, SPL/PR*

CHAPTER 4
*p.62—© David Young-Wolff/PhotoEdit   p.63—© Dr. Charles R. Belinky/PR
p.64—© G&H SOHO   p.67—© Robert Brenner/PhotoEdit   p.69—© George Holton/PR
p.71—© CMSP   p.72—© Myrleen Ferguson/PhotoEdit   p.77—© Ken Lax/PR*

CHAPTER 5
*p.81—© Jean Kenndy, SPL/Science Source   p.82—© CMSP/SPL   p.85—© Yoav Levy/Phototake
NYC   p.86—© Amy C. Etra/PhotoEdit   p.88—© Françoise Sauze, SPL/PR   p.90—© Sheila
Terry, SPL/PR   p.91—© Michael Newman/PhotoEdit   p.94—© Tony Freeman/PhotoEdit
p.97—© Will and Deni McIntyre/PR*

CHAPTER 6
*p.104—© Prof. P. Motta/Dept. of Anatomy/University "La Sapienza," Rome, SPL/PR
p.105—© Ulrike Welsch/PhotoEdit   p.106—© Alexander Tsiaras, SPL/PR   p.107—© Michael
Newman/PhotoEdit   p.111—© CDC/Phototake NYC   p.113—© CMSP   p.115—© Jerry
Wachter/PR*

CHAPTER 7
*p.117—© Robert Brenner/Phototake   p.119—© Tom Prettyman/PhotoEdit
p.121—© Mark Richards/PhotoEdit   p.123—© David Young-Wolff/PhotoEdit
p.124—© Courtesy Jim Harris   p.126—© Eunice Harris/PR   p.131—© M. Ferguson/PhotoEdit*